LAW AND BUREAUCRACY

JEFFREY L. JOWELL

LAW AND BUREAUCRACY

Administrative Discretion and the Limits of Legal Action

DUNELLEN PUBLISHING COMPANY, INC.

Distributed exclusively by Kennikat Press, Port Washington, New York

Manufactured in the United States of America

Distributed by
Kennikat Press, 90 South Bayles Avenue, Port Washington, N. Y. 11050

European and UK Distribution by
Martin Robertson, Ltd., London

University Press of Cambridge, Mass. Series in
the Social Sciences. Eugene H. Nellen, Editor.

Library of Congress Cataloging in Publication Data

Jowell, Jeffrey L
    Law and bureaucracy.

    (University Press of Cambridge, Mass. series in the
social sciences)
    Includes bibliographical references and index.
    1. Administrative discretion—United States.
2. Administrative discretion—Boston. I. Title.
KF5407.J6   342'.73'066   75–33893
ISBN 0-8046-7098-6

Contents

Acknowledgments

This study could not have been conducted without free access to the three agencies studied. I am grateful for permission for this access to the then-heads of these agencies: Mal Webber of the Massachusetts Commission Against Discrimination, Daniel Cronin of the Boston Department of Welfare, and Edward Logue of the Boston Redevelopment Authority. I am grateful too to the people working in these agencies for tolerating my interruption of their work routine with frequent requests for files or information. Head Social Work Supervisor, Frances Sullivan, at the Roxbury Crossing Office of the Welfare Department, and Commissioners Ruth Batson and Ben Shapiro at the Massachusetts Commission Against Discrimination were particularly patient in this regard.

The structured interviews were conducted by Harvard Student Agencies Research Service, and by Community Research Project of Metropolitan Boston. I am indebted to Morris Axelrod of Community Research Project for his thoroughness and help with the drafting of the questionnaire and the coding of data. Martin Whyte gave me needed assistance with the computer work and the interpretation of data.

Sadelle Sacks and the staff at Fair Housing, Incorporated, were perhaps in greater contact with the problems considered in this paper than anyone. Mrs. Sacks's kindness and willingness to share her experience and information is highly appreciated.

For advice and thoughtful criticism of aspects of this work as it developed I am extremely grateful to Professors Albert Sacks, Edward Banfield, Lon Fuller, Adam Yarmolinsky and Talcott Parsons. Chad Gordon instructed me in research method. John Hogarth, Paul Weiler and Tom Wilson provided perceptive and helpful comments on earlier drafts.

Pam Hodges, Margaret Goble and Noella Allen typed the manuscript and gave invaluable and greatly appreciated assistance.

I am particularly grateful to the Joint Center for Urban Studies of Harvard and M.I.T. for a V.O. Key fellowship, which gave me research facilities and an enriching year with stimulating colleagues.

Despite this help, and other generous support from individuals in the Boston area, the shortcomings in this study are mine alone.

J.L.J.

London, 1975

LAW AND BUREAUCRACY

Introduction

Administrative bodies, styled impersonally as boards, commissions, departments, authorities and so on, constitute a major mechanism for decision in our society. Many of their decisions may affect issues as basic as whether a family will or will not receive enough food to eat on a given weekend, whether a mother will or will not be permitted to send her son to a school for the handicapped, or whether a family will be forced to leave their home. The decisions are in fact taken by individual officials—human beings occupying a place in an organization. The legally trained Max Weber told us that bureaucracy in its ideal type embodies a legalistic purity, where officials are subject to strict systematic control and discipline and enforce the law "without hatred or passion and hence without affection or enthusiasm."[1] In reality, however, the power of the police, welfare officials, planners and a host of other officials often allows decision and action according to a high degree of discretion, relatively free of legal control.

The literature on the administrative process is growing with critical appraisals advocating that administration be subject to constraint through law. Some of the critics strike a note of impatience; they feel that administrative agencies are there to clarify standards that the legislature was unable or unwilling to make anything but vague. The critics want the administration therefore to cease their "aimless drifting"[2] and "procrastination."[3] It is argued that the effort of standard-clarification will itself shake an agency into awareness of its real task, and force it to "focus on issues previously only dimly perceived."[4]

The recent works of Charles Reich and Kenneth Culp Davis have been particularly influential in their proposals for the legal control of administration. Reich, in a series of articles,[5] outlines the growth of government largesse, those increasingly frequent situations where individuals receive privileges from the state, and are therefore at the mercy and subject to the control of official discretion. In the area of welfare law, for example, Reich favors granting to recipients firm "rights" or "entitlement" under criteria established in advance, or through the protection of full adjudicatory procedures.

Davis admits that some discretion is necessary, but is concerned with the amount of "unnecessary discretion" wielded at all levels of administration, which provides opportunity for administrators to depart from official policy. He suggests the use of precise rules to "confine" discretion—set its boundaries and shave it down to a minimum compatible with the effective exercise of the task to be performed, or to "structure" discretion—channel it to take cognizance of officially-sanctioned criteria. Davis also suggests that where possible discretion should be "checked" by persons other than the decision maker, and "structured" in such a way as to be "open," that is, exposed to public scrutiny—through open plans, open policy statements, open rules, open findings, open reasons, open precedents and fair, informal procedures.

The primary purpose of this study is to consider the extent to which bureaucracy can (or cannot) be controlled by legal techniques, can be "legalized," or "judicialized." Although these terms are frequently used interchangeably,[6] "legalization" will refer here to the process of subjecting official decision to the governance of predetermined rules, and

2

"judicialization" will refer to the process of submitting official decision to adjudicative procedures. The term "bureaucracy" will not refer here strictly to Weber's ideal type. Nor will it, or the term "bureaucrat," intend the pejorative connotation frequently implied colloquially. The term will be used interchangeably with "administrative agency" or "organization" and will refer to a system of consciously coordinated activities on the part of two or more persons for the achievement of administrative objectives.[7]

In seeking an answer to the question of the role of law on bureaucracy, the operation of three agencies in the city of Boston was examined. This enables the work to pursue a secondary theme, following the path taken by law as it is shone into and through bureaucracy, and considering whether the path emerges where it was aimed (insofar as we can determine the initial direction), or whether it is refracted in the course of its journey. We shall attempt to open the "black box" of bureaucracy in order to note the forces that may cause any such refraction. The research method will thus allow some examination of the problems involved in achieving a social purpose through the instrument of law mediated by bureaucracy. In addition, the substantive and procedural law in three areas—welfare, race discrimination and urban renewal—will be considered.

The arrangement of this work will take the following form: Chapter 1 sets out the arguments in abstract concerning the legal control of bureaucracy, and considers the merits and defects of rules and adjudication as techniques of social decision and devices to control decision making. In this connection it was found helpful to bring together literature not only from works of jurisprudence concerning the judicial decision, but also from those dealing with the sociology of organizations and public administration, since legal theory largely fails to consider material about the law of organizations, and about the behavior of men in organizations.

Having considered these questions in the abstract, the study then proceeds to consider concrete experience which is drawn from the operations of three administrative agencies in the city of Boston. The agencies are: The Boston Department of Public Welfare, the Massachusetts Commission Against Discrimination, and the Boston Redevelopment Authority. Access to them was considered necessary in order to gain insight into the operations of bureaucracy and the attitudes of their personnel and clientele in one city (Boston) at one point of time (late 1960's), for the purpose of testing hypotheses advanced in this study and elsewhere in the literature.[8]

One hypothesis that it is sought to test extensively is that utilization of legal rights varies according to the group for whose benefit the law exists. For example, large corporations may make frequent use of the law, but a welfare mother may for a variety of reasons be unable or unwilling to utilize any legal rights that she may have. This point may seem obvious, but it is frequently lost, particularly by well-meaning lawyers who state emphatically that "there ought to be a law" or "there ought to be rights." The agencies drawn upon to test this hypothesis are thus in many ways unrepresentative of the federal commissions that form the traditional grist for researchers' mills, for the reason at least that they serve urban clientele who are mostly poor, or members of minority racial groups.

Chapters 2 to 4 consider this question of access to law and bureaucracy in an attempt to clarify where obstacles to access may lie, who they may affect, and why. The three agencies present three different situations of how access may be gained: The first situation involves a complaint to bureaucracy about a previous official decision. Here the complaint of a welfare recipient about her caseworker's determination to the Boston Public Welfare Board of Appeals is considered (in chapter 2). The second situation involves a complaint to bureaucracy about a private wrong. Here the complaint of racial discrimination to the Massachusetts Commission Against Discrimination is considered (in chapter 3). The third situation involves access that *prima facie* appears to be the responsibility of bureaucracy itself to initiate. Here the requirement of "citizen participation" in urban renewal is considered (in chapter 4), through an examination of an urban renewal project conducted by the Boston Redevelopment Authority in the Madison Park area of Boston's Roxbury.

Before considering the implications of the findings about the limits to access, a further limit to law is explored (in chapter 5) namely, that it is not capable of solving certain problems, or, conversely, that certain tasks are not amenable to legal control. The question of "need" in welfare is seen to be the kind of problem that is ideally unsuited to resolution by "legal" decision. A model is presented which, it is suggested, more realistically explains administrative tasks than the usual "rule-making-adjudication" dichotomy, and allows us to understand the necessary role of discretion. Chapter 6 attempts to discover what constraints and what influences in fact operate upon bureaucracy. The operations of the Massachusetts Commission Against Discrimination are analyzed, and the necessary role of discretion, and necessary scope for political influence, observed.

In the light of the limited access to law and bureaucracy, the functional limits of legal control over bureaucratic decision-making, and the necessary role of discretion and political influence, the study concludes with suggestions about the respective place of discretion, legal control and advocacy in the administrative process. These conclusions probably provide only limited encouragement to those who favor greater legal control of administrative decision-making, but they are presented in the hope that a recognition of the limits of legal action ought to allow a more useful exploitation of its potential.

RESEARCH METHOD

Any examination of the administrative process provides an

immediate problem of perspective: whose construction of the reality of the situation ought to be accepted?

The ideal objective of an organization can be gleaned to some extent from its legal structure, as explained by its legislative history. However, the initial purposes may have been vague, or conflicting; and perhaps initial purposes have become obsolete, or have changed over time. Another source for gaining knowledge of the ideal objectives might therefore be the officials who are in charge of attaining these objectives. On the other hand, they may tailor their view of the ideal by what is in reality capable of achievement. Individuals actually or potentially affected by an organization's operations (its clientele) may also possess a view of the ideal objectives and means of achieving that ideal.

The real achievements of an organization are also often incapable of objective assessment. How do we know that an anti-discrimination commission is succeeding in its objective of reducing racial discrimination in the community (assuming this as its one identifiable objective)? Do we take as an index of success the fact that the number of complaints to the commission have risen in the past year? Have diminished in the past year? That more complaints have proved justifiable? That fewer complaints have proved justifiable? Or should we ask the average black person his opinion of the extent of discrimination in society? Or his opinion of the role of the commission?

In undertaking research for this study, the problem of perspective was borne in mind. It was realized that an "objective" view of organizational objectives and achievements was unlikely to be possible. Therefore, an attempt was made to view the situation from three vantage points. The first is the "paper" content of the organizations; that is, the governing statute, their own rules (substantive and procedural), and case results as reflected in their files and statistics. The second point of assessment is the "official" point of view. The personnel of the three agencies were interviewed (informally, at times in the course of work routine) and observed, in an attempt to understand the organizational objectives from their point of view, and also to know the constraints under which they considered themselves to be operating. Finally, an attempt was made to view the organizational process from the perspective of the clientele of the organization; those persons within an organization's jurisdiction to the extent that they fall within the ambit of its powers (like residents of an urban renewal area presided over by The Boston Redevelopment Authority) or are beneficiaries of its operations (like potential or actual recipients of welfare dispensed by the Boston Department of Public Welfare).

It is not suggested that we can fit these three perspectives together and thereby gain a truly objective view of the whole. It is suggested that the organizational enterprise involves a process, and that an understanding of the process requires, at least, a recognition of the different interests and perspectives of the actors in the process.

The study of the Boston Department of Public Welfare was conducted from March 1967 to March 1968. The author was given access to the case records of all appeal hearings heard during that time at one District Office. All seventy hearings were attended in person. To obtain information about the welfare process other than the appeal hearings, the case files were read back to the time of the recipient's first application for welfare assistance (in some cases back about ten years, in others only one month). During the year other aspects of the welfare process were observed, including home-visits and intake applications. Numerous unstructured interviews and conversations were held with caseworkers, appeal referees, and social work supervisors.

The study of the Massachusetts Commission Against Discrimination was conducted during 1966 and was based on a reading of all cases laid at the Boston Office during 1965 alleging racial discrimination in housing and employment. While in the office, the case-analysis was supplemented by unstructured interviews and conversations with the Commission's staff, including field representatives, the Reseach Director, the Executive Secretary and all the Commissioners.

The study of the Boston Redevelopment Authority focuses on one project conducted by the agency in the Madison Park area of Boston's Roxbury. The Project Director of that and three other urban renewal projects, as well as other members of the BRA staff, were interviewed. The Madison Park hearing before the Boston City Council was observed personally, and the participants interviewed informally.

The attitudes of the clientele of all these agencies were sought through structured interviews conducted in February and March 1968 by professional interviewers. Blacks and whites were interviewed by members of their own race. The interviews lasted from thirty to sixty minutes.[9] The data obtained was analyzed employing a packaged computer program called data-text.[10] The following were interviewed:

1. A random sample of forty-two welfare appellants—about two thirds of those who laid appeals at the District Office during the year. Half of this sample was black, half white—a racial composition which approximated that of the total number of appellants, although selected randomly.
2. A random sample of thirty-five MCAD complainants—about forty per cent of those who laid housing complaints before the MCAD in 1965.
3. A random sample of one hundred and three adult members of Madison Park who had been living in the area from the start of the project activity in mid-1966. The sample represented approximately half of the residences in the area at the time of the survey, and was composed of forty whites and sixty-three blacks—a racial composition reflecting approximately that of the area, although selected randomly.

Each person interviewed was asked questions about the agency of which he was a client, in addition to questions about the other agencies. For example, respondents in Madison Park were asked primarily about the Madison Park urban renewal area. However, if black, they were asked questions about anti-discrimination laws and the MCAD. They were also asked questions relating to welfare.

The Madison Park area is situated in Boston's Roxbury area, which in 1960 consisted of a racial composition that was 57 per cent white and 43 per cent black, although over seventeen census tracts were more than half black.[11] Madison Park was one of these. At the time of the present survey, 60 per cent of the households were black, 40 per cent white.[12] Like other areas in Roxbury, Madison Park was an area of comparatively recent black influx, and white outflow. Those whites who had remained in the area were older than the average black; 70 per cent of the whites, but only 38 per cent of the blacks were older than fifty years of age. The area is one of Boston's poorest. The median family income level in 1968 was $3,200, less than half of the Boston median in 1960 of $6,687. The median income level for blacks was $3,180, substantially lower than the 1960 black median of $4,447.[13] About a third of the sample were receiving welfare.

It is hoped that the reader will bear in mind the frequently small sample size and the dangers of generalizing from attitudes revealed in formal, impersonal interviews. The data is employed here to supplement information gained through the first-hand case studies of the agencies, and is only suggestive or illustrative of propositions raised.

Notes

1. M. Weber, *The Theory of Social and Economic Organization*, Trans. A. Henderson and T. Parsons, at 340, (1947).
2. H. Friendly, *The Federal Administrative Agencies: The Need for a Better Definition of Standards*, at 24 (1962).
3. K. C. Davis, *Discretionary Justice, a Preliminary Inquiry*, at 56 (1969).
4. D. Shapiro, "The Choice of Rulemaking and Adjudication in the Development of Administrative Policy", 78 *Harv. L. Rev.* 921,941 (1965).
5. C. Reich, "The New Property," 73 *Yale L.J.* 773 (1964); "Midnight Welfare Searches and the Social Security Act," 72 *Yale L.J.* 1347 (1963); "Individual Rights and Social Welfare: The Emerging Issues," 74 *Yale L.J.* 1245 (1965); "The Law of the Planned Society," 75 *Yale L.J.* 1227 (1966).
6. e.g. by P. Nonet, *Administrative Justice* (1969); P. Selznick, *Law, Society and Industrial Justice* (1969).
7. This definition combines Peter Blau's definition of bureaucracy [*The Dynamics of Bureaucracy*, at 251 (1955)] and Chester Barnard's definition of organization [*The Functions of the Executive*, at 73 (1938).]
8. Only a few and recent studies have considered the interaction between law and bureaucracy at the local level, or through the approach of a case-study. Those that have done so will be drawn on frequently here. Some of these are: L. Mayhew, *Law And Equal Opportunity* (1968); P. Nonet, *op. cit.*, J. Q. Wilson, *Varieties of Police Behavior* (1968) and the articles of Joel Handler to be cited below.
9. The questionnaires may be obtained from the author, at cost.
10. A. Couch, *The Data-Text System* (1966).
11. U.S. Dept. of Commerce, *Census of Housing*, vol. 1, part 4 (1960).
12. These figures and others cited here were computed by generalizing from the sample interviewed in Madison Park and confirmed by a survey carried out by the Boston Redevelopment Authority in March to May, 1966. In that survey 158 of 384 existing households were interviewed. Boston Redevelopment Authority, *Diagnostic Report, Residents of the Proposed Campus High School Early Land Acquisition Area* (1966).
13. U.S. Dept. of Commerce, *Census of Population*, Vol. 1, part 23 (1960).

1

The Legal Control of Bureaucracy

Law has been defined as "the enterprise of subjecting human conduct to the governance of rules."[1] The advocates of "legalization" of the administrative process would, similarly, transform policies—broad statements of general objectives—into rules—authoritative general directions that contain relatively specific and concrete guides for decision.[2] Thus the administration of a law intended to prevent unsafe driving would be progressively "legalized" as all elements of "unsafe" driving were reduced to specific rules—for example, maximum speed limits and one-way streets.

The advocates of rule-controlled administration are at times fervent in their belief. Davis, for example, calls rule making "one of the great inventions of modern government."[3] Before proceeding to case studies of actual bureaucratic operations, this chapter will consider in abstract the reasons for and against predetermined rules, definiteness of standards, and the confining of discretion, as variously described, as a technique of controlling official discretion. The merits and defects of another legal technique of discretion control, "judicialization" (defined here as the process of submitting official decisions to adjudicative procedures), will also be considered.

THE MERITS OF RULES

The Rule of Law, "Extravagant Version"

The first argument for rules governing administrative discretion reflects a political philosophy that rejects unlimited freedom for the administrative decision maker who is not subject to direct accountability to the electorate. Rules are thus seen as a means of both reducing the free exercise of discretion and providing specific standards against which official decisions may be measured. Where there is no congruence between rule and decision, affected persons could hold officials accountable through challenge by judicial review. The adherents of this view, which Davis terms the "extravagant version of the rule of law,"[4] maintain therefore that administrative action, however benignly exercised, should always be subject to predetermined rules and judicial challenge.

When argued from the perspective of persons affected by administrative action, the extravagant version of the rule of law maintains that conduct ought to be subject to predetermined rules that will be uniformly applied by officials to all "like" cases. Justice will thus be done in two senses—first, as between two or more like-situationed parties, who will be treated uniformly, and second, to the extent that persons will not be punished by rules applied *ex post facto*.

The extravagant version of the rule of law thus rests upon a political philosophy and a concept of justice. However, it considers neither the content of rules, the relation of the existence of a rule to the nature of the task to be performed, nor the effect of rules upon the substantive outcome of decisions. Nonetheless, the "extravagant" argument does contain desirable features. Accountability, uniformity of application and the prospective application of rules are important ideals toward which all administration ought to strive.[5] In addition, from a purely practical perspective, a minimum of predetermined knowledge of the legality of our actions is necessary in modern society.[6] We need to know, for example, the permissible range of speed and permissible parking places.

Those with business interests need reliable rules in order to achieve certainty and predictability in their operations. Because they are involved in planning and allocating often considerable resources, they could rarely afford to take action that might later be curtailed or prohibited. Business is always more confidently undertaken in an atmosphere of certainty; given the lack of predictability of so many other factors—for example, consumer demand, or supply of investment capital and labor—business considers the stability of operating ground rules particularly desirable.

The argument for certain and predictable rules is powerful. However, it does not in any way address itself to the substantive outcome of official decisions. No part of the extravagant version requires that rules be good rules. As Mr. Justice Brandeis said, "It is usually more important that a rule of law be settled than that it be settled right."[7]

The Integrity of Administration

Rules could be used to influence substantive administrative decisions by encouraging "congruence"[8] between officially determined ends and official action, particularly by excluding or reducing the possibility of arbitrary decisions.[9] Dean Pound alluded to the use of "strict rules" to achieve this purpose since

they secure us against the well meant ignorance or feebleness of will of the weak judge and are our mainstay against improper motives on the part of those who administer justice.[10]

13

As articulated policies, rules could also have the effect of increasing administrative accountability to the public.

Congruence Between Officially Determined Objectives and Official Action. Official objectives are sometimes not clear, and they may change over time.[11] As will be considered fully later,[12] an organization charged with implementing vague legislation will itself be an agent in the clarification and elaboration of legislative policies. In this sense, bureaucracies are law makers themselves (Weber's picture of mechanical enforcement notwithstanding). Nevertheless, rules may provide a means to ensure that the "line bureaucrat" performs in accordance with official policy, as defined either by the legislature or by the bureaucracy itself.[13] Rules are thus devices to eliminate some of the refractory elements that cause the distortion of official ends during the course of the administrative process.

The main culprit in the distortion process is the arbitrary decision, which is defined here as one based upon improper criteria[14] that do not relate in any rational way to organizational ends. The paradigm arbitrary decision is one based upon particularistic criteria such as friendship, or ascriptive criteria such as race, or upon caprice, whim, or prejudice.

The question of a decision's arbitrariness frequently arises in the context of the "selective enforcement" (or nonenforcement) of laws.[15] For example, police enforce a law selectively when they arrest (assuming this power) speeders on street A but not on street B. Selective enforcement may frequently be a function of limited resources. Because there are, for example, a limited number of police patrolmen, they could not between them possibly detect and apprehend every speeder. Therefore they utilize their scarce resources most effectively by patrolling one particular street or by stopping only those vehicles that exceed the maximum speed limit by more than five miles per hour; perhaps they might stop one of every four speeders.

Selective enforcement is often resented by the person

against whom the law is enforced. The one person who is fined for speeding considers it unjust that three other speeding cars were ignored. However, full enforcement of the traffic laws is not physically possible. Furthermore, as will be shown later, selective enforcement can also be a technique to mitigate the harshness that might flow from strict enforcement.

Continuing our illustration, police discretion moves toward the arbitrary (arbitrariness is a matter of degree) when the police patrolman, instead of randomly selecting one of every four speeding cars, stratifies his sample and arrests only long-haired drivers of speeding blue cars. The decision would be clearly arbitrary should the police officer arrest black speeders alone, or desist from arresting a speeder who is a friend or relative or has offered him a bribe. Such criteria for not invoking the criminal process (race, friendship) are not rationally related to the organizational ends (preventing unsafe driving) and are generally accepted to be improper.

The use of improper criteria that may be rationally related to official ends will make a decision nonarbitrary (e.g., if customs officials search only long-haired youths for illicit drugs, when a positive correlation between long-haired youth and drug use could be assumed). Similarly, a mistaken decision would not be arbitrary per se even though its effect was not related to organizational ends (e.g., a police officer's decision to arrest a driver traveling at 57 miles per hour where the police officer had believed the driver to be exceeding the 55 mile per hour maximum speed limit).[16]

The arbitrary decision should also be distinguished from a "legalistic" one. For example, a police officer's decision to arrest a person who exceeded the speed limit by one mile per hour on a deserted road in the early hours of the morning would surely not be rationally related to the objectives of the laws regarding safe driving, although it is quite proper by legal standards.[17] Legalism is thus the prim relative of the unruly arbitrary; they share the quality of a lack of rational relation between the action taken and the ends to be

15

achieved. However, whereas the arbitrary motive is improper, the motive for legalistic action, namely, to be within the letter of the law, is impeccably, if narrowly, correct.

Rules could thus aid in removing decision-making criteria that are either improper in themselves or unrelated to organizational ends. We have seen that in many cases, but not all, improper criteria will be unrelated to ends. But difficult value judgments would have to be made concerning the propriety of the conduct of the customs official who searches only long-haired youths, or the conduct of a police officer who agrees to release a randomly apprehended speeder who provides the police officer with the *quid pro quo* of information that could lead to a third party's arrest. The police officer's action is clearly related to his organizational ends, namely, law enforcement; but the question whether the action is proper is more difficult to answer.

These questions will be considered again. For the present, we may note that rules could be utilized to prohibit the use of certain clearly improper and particularistic criteria. For example, rules might specifically exclude as criteria for determining whether an applicant was "suitable" or "desirable" for a public housing tenancy factors such as the applicant's race, his previous membership in certain political organizations, his previous participation in tenant rent strikes, or his relationship to other tenants or to an official.

Alternatively, rules could explicitly prescribe certain objective decision-making criteria, by implication excluding those that might be improper. For example, criteria for eligibility for welfare or public housing could be a stated minimum income level, or a criterion for worker benefits or promotion could be seniority.

Finally, rules might be used to inhibit the possibility of decisions being based upon incorrect interpretations of official objectives. For example, although the broad objectives of public-housing laws are to provide housing for the poor, families without an adult head, mothers who give birth to illegitimate children, or persons who have previous criminal records are evicted or rejected by housing authorities as undesirables.[18] Rules could (within limits considered below) correct situations such as these, which might deprive those who are most poor, or most in need, of accommodation in public housing. The method to achieve this would again be either specifically to exclude such criteria, or specifically to list criteria for selection or eviction that are consonant with officially determined objectives.

Administrative Accountability. Once policies are taken out from under the ambit of discretionary application and exposed as rules, they are no longer hidden from public scrutiny. In part, the argument for the "rights" of welfare recipients rests on a desire to remove a recipient's grant from the status of a privilege to be awarded at the discretion of the case worker to that of rule-established entitlement. A rule is formal notice of entitlement; should a case worker refuse to comply with the rule, he could be held legally accountable by the wronged recipient.

At first sight, this argument resembles the extravagant version of the rule of law because it calls for administrative accountability to predetermined rule, without specifying what the effect or the content of the rule might be, or its appropriateness for the task in hand.[19] However, two recent contributions to the literature suggest that legalization itself might affect the substance of rules.

In his study of the administration of workman's compensation laws, Nonet sees legalization (the transformation of policies into rules) itself as an opportunity for gaining recognition of substantive rights in administrative programs.[20] Nonet considers the legal order to have its own "built-in principles of criticism."[21] He states that once an administrator becomes accountable to rule, both criticism and the emphasis on entitlement make the content of the rules themselves an issue for debate. The rules then become subject to "conditional support by reasoned argument and persuasion."[22]

Selznick pursues the same theme in his study of industrial

relations and the law.[23] Citing the example of a modern university, he asserts that the legalization of student-faculty rights[24] does not simply allow university officials to "congratulate themselves—and await obedience."[25] The new rules generate a critical spirit, which entails a scrutiny both of the integrity of the rules' administration *and* the quality of the rules themselves. The rules are thus assessed "in the light of substantive ends."[26]

Another aspect of rules that is claimed to induce administrative accountability and responsiveness to affected parties involves the process of making rules.[27] This claim is normally made in opposition to adjudication as an administrative decision-making technique. Whereas adjudication allows consultation of the litigating parties alone, rule making allows notice and opportunity for comment to all affected parties.[28] We have seen that an authority of K. C. Davis' stature considers the rule-making procedure to be one of the greatest inventions of modern government. He is referring chiefly to the federal Administrative Procedure Act, which provides for publishing proposed rules and inviting interested parties to make written comments.[29] Without yet considering the possible demerits of rule making, we might note that even under the act the procedures outlined above do not apply to "interpretative rules," "general statements of policy,"[30] and other exceptions.[31] Nevertheless, an open, consultative rule making process, where it applies or may be introduced, may well act as an effective control on administrative discretion, and may also provoke the on-going process of scrutiny and criticism that Nonet and Selznick suggest will help render administrative responsiveness to affected interests.

Administrative Advantages of Rules

Many who would wish to constrain administrative discretion by rules tend to assume that administrative organizations, in their quest to maintain and enhance their status, or freedom of action, would naturally oppose legal constraints on their discretion. This reaction might prove true in some cases. It will be argued below that the degree of opposition to legalization is most likely to depend upon the task being performed and the political situation in which the organization in question is operating. There are also, however, compelling reasons which might lead administration to favor reducing its own discretion by rules. These will now be considered.

Planning and Routinization. Business convenience is seen as being furthered by certain and predictable rules, which will serve as guides to facilitate planning. Public organizations as well as business organizations are involved in the allocation of scarce resources. A welfare department, for example, disburses a limited budget to demanding clients. The formulation of rules in advance of specific claims would allow the department rationally to estimate the projected demands upon its supply of resources. Rules would then serve to regulate both the eligible demand (specifying, e.g., maximum income and capital levels above which an applicant would not be eligible for welfare) and the supply of allowable resources (e.g., by limiting grants to a maximum for any specified category, or by prohibiting certain special grants or special grants above a stated maximum).

Rules, of course, are guides to more efficient handling of cases. Mass transactions almost always require routinized treatment. Attempting to weigh the merits of each case *de novo* would, in many situations, be an insupportable investment of administrative time. For example, housing inspectors charged with the enforcement of minimum codes could decide whether a house is "substandard" on a case-by-case basis. Realistically, however, the inspector must refer to a minimum of predetermined rules—a checklist of objective criteria against which each dwelling may, fairly, be measured. If a criterion can be quantified (e.g., temperature no lower than 70° F. in winter), so much the better.

19

All announced rules possess administrative benefits to the extent that they allow affected persons to know them (subject to the major qualification that rules are frequently imperfectly communicated). Rules therefore announce or clarify official policies to affected parties, thus facilitating obedience.

Rules as Shields. For the conscientious administrator, making decisions unguided by defined standards or rules requires the constant re-examination of basic premises in the light of new conditions. Of course, some administrators might be happy to take the line of least resistance, to follow the argument where the strongest pressures lead, and to repeat past decisions without bothering to distinguish facts or reappraise premises. But if most administrators tend to fall into fixed decision-making patterns, it is in part because they, like all men, possess limited energy, limited intellectual resources, and a limited capacity to engage daily the pressures thrust upon them. Rules to guide decisions will often be welcomed as a device to conserve energy and to protect officials from undue tensions and pressures.

Constant mental energy is required to assess the "needs" of every welfare recipient or the "substandardness" of every house examined (assuming that these concepts can be appropriately assessed at all). It is relatively easy to have a checklist against which to measure objective characteristics (e.g., date of last grant of a winter coat, age, number of children). The adjectives used to describe the application of rules include "impersonal," "mechanical," "disinterested," "objective"; they all suggest the exclusion of human or affective considerations. Max Weber's portrayal of the ideal-typical bureaucratic official applying rules *"sine ira et studio*—without hatred or passion, and hence without affection or enthusiasm,"[32] alludes ‎to the low anxiety factor involved in rule-application. To the decision maker, a rule might therefore "reduce headaches"[33] and provide relief from the tension of having to decide each case anew without the benefit of authoritative guidance.

Rules also tend to insulate the decision maker from political pressures. It will be argued later that administration is by no means exempt from political pressures, particularly where discretion is high. Clearly, the greater the freedom of a decision maker's choice, the greater will be the opportunity for affected parties to influence the choice. A rule, however, provides the decision maker with an authoritative excuse to stand firm. Where the rule has been enacted through a process of participatory consultation, its legitimacy is enhanced. James Q. Wilson points out, for example, that when police officials want to take the police "out of politics,"

The most obvious way to achieve this is to assert that there is a clear difference between law-givers and law-enforcers or, more generally, between policy and administration. Every police officer likes to remark, "We don't make the laws" in dealing with an angry housewife who has received a ticket or whose son has been arrested; it is a conventional observation intended obviously to reduce interpersonal conflict by representing the police officer as the impersonal and slightly sympathetic agent of a remote "Law."[34]

Rules may open an agency to more rigorous accountability.[35] But they also provide an effective political shield behind which officials may hide, safe in the knowledge that in response to pressures they have a valid reply: "I'd like to help you, but I'm bound by this rule."

THE DEFECTS OF RULES

Much of what we have just considered to be advantages of rules will be contradicted by what follows. The two positions are not reconcilable. They are not meant to be. Rules possess merits and demerits—in the abstract. A major thesis of this

21

study is that the argument for or against legalization should not be pursued in the abstract, but in the light of the particular task to be performed, and in the knowledge that the perspective of the actor (official or public) often determines the perception of rules as a merit or defect.

Rigidity and Legalism

When bureaucracy is charged with the application of rules, organizational routines are set in motion whenever a set of categorized facts occur. We have seen that some problems must be solved by a minimum of routine handling through the categorization of data. The effect of this is to reduce the personality both of the official and of the affected client who is seen as a "carrier of data" relevant to the task at hand.[36] He is thus a "complainant of discrimination," a "welfare applicant," a "speeder." Weber's "objective" discharge of business "without regard to persons"[37] thus occurs.

On the other hand, all persons who come into contact with rules will have noted that, as categorizing general directions, rules may easily catch within their ambit technical violators whose actions have not contravened the objectives of the enforcing bureaucracy. For example, a parking meter will not show understanding or mercy to the person who was one minute over the limit because he was helping a blind man cross the street. Rules thus permit legalism, which, because of its close affinity to arbitrariness (i.e., lack of rational relation to official ends), may cause dissatisfaction on the part of technical violators.

However understandable his breach of a parking by-law may have been, the rule categorizes the person who helped the blind man as a violator of the law. Nor is the rule able to justify this. Unlike a reasoned adjudicative decision, rules do not carry with them any explanations (apart from the occasional vague preamble of a statute and insofar as they may receive judicial elaboration). For example, nothing in the rule itself explains to a welfare recipient why she may be permitted, as a "special need," a washing machine, but not a television set or dishwasher.[38]

Furthermore, the content of rules varies. The advocates of rules *qua* rules tend to assume that all rules are good rules. Commentators have proposed, for example, that rules should specify criteria for eviction from public housing, thus giving tenants certain specified "rights."[39] If the rules are intended to prohibit improper and arbitrary conduct, then the case for rules is sound. However, rules may impose hardships—for example, insisting that a welfare recipient bring a support action against her husband, or prohibiting public housing tenants from keeping pets. As Lawrence Friedman has pointed out:

It is so easy to forbid pets—a stroke of the pen will do it. It is not quite so easy to calculate the costs and the benefits of cats and dogs and to try to devise some method of letting tenants have their pets without harming the project.[40]

Rules, therefore, permit official behavior that may show no apparent relation between fidelity to the rule and organizational ends. However, techniques to temper strict rule-enforcement do exist. One judicial technique is the imposition of a nominal penalty (where a rule imposing a minimum penalty does not exist) or nominal damages. An administrative technique is selective enforcement or nonenforcement allowing, for example, a police officer to refrain from fining a doctor speeding to the scene of an accident, or a driver narrowly exceeding a speed limit in the early hours of the morning. But, as we have seen, selective enforcement creates as many problems as it solves and is only possible where the administrator has the opportunity to refrain from setting legal enforcement in motion.

We shall see the apparent legalism of rules relating to welfare need, where, in a manner that appears nonrational, a caseworker has no power to grant a recipient a nonallowable dishwasher in place of the allowed clothes washer. It would be a bold public housing administrator who exempted from a prohibition against dogs the Seeing Eye dog of a blind tenant.[41]

Organization theorists have pointed out certain legalistic tendencies within organizations that arise from ritualistic attachment to routines and procedures. Victor Thompson refers to these patterns as "bureaupathic," because they do not advance organizational goals but rather reflect the status needs of individuals in the organization.[42] Rules are used by superordinates to control subordinates, who in turn go strictly "by the book," follow precedent, and avoid innovations or chances of error by developing an exaggerated dependence upon regulations and quantitative standards:

Everybody, including the supervisor, is simply carrying out instructions imposed from above. If they are unpleasant instructions, it is not the supervisor's fault. . . .[43]

These remarks, from the intraorganizational perspective, reflect a propensity among officials to hide behind a rule. The need on their part for routinization and protection from the continuing obligation of discretionary decision is understandable. "Bureaupathic" behavior, however, within an organization or between an organization and its clientele, bears no relation to organizational ends.[44]

To the client, therefore, the official refuge behind rules might be seen as an excuse to ignore valid claims. The obligation of a reasoned decision *de novo*, while not guaranteeing the absence of official ignorance or prejudice, constitutes at least some protection against the mechanical application of rules in situations that do not further rational objectives; at best it provides an assurance of personal attention, and "individualized justice." The administrator might also prefer to look at each case anew, and to preserve the flexibility that a rule may preclude.

ADJUDICATION

The second technique proposed by advocates of the legal control of the administrative process is the use of adjudicatory procedures. Charles Reich wants welfare rights to be determined by means of the usual protections and participation of affected interests that surround this method of institutional decision making.[45]

The concept of adjudication adopted here will closely follow Lon Fuller's. Fuller has defined adjudication as "a social process of decision which assures to the affected party a particular form of participation, that of presenting proofs and arguments for a decision in his favor."[46] Adjudication is thus a means of institutionally guaranteed participation because each party to the dispute may present proofs and arguments. Other institutionally guaranteed means of participation are, for example, elections, where the means of participation is the vote, and contracts, where the means of participation is negotiation.

The main consequence of Fuller's concept of adjudication is the restraint associated with the judicial role. The proofs and arguments of the litigants ought to be presented to an impartial and unbiased decision maker. The decision maker should not hold private conferences with either party, otherwise the excluded party may not know to what issue he should direct his proofs and arguments. Each party should have the opportunity to cross-examine the other.

In addition, adjudication implies what might be called functional prerequisites. For a decision to be amenable to resolution by adjudication, the decision maker must be able to reach a decision on the basis of some rule, standard, or principle that is generalizable and applicable to all future "like" cases. This prerequisite flows from the method of institutional participation because, for a participant to present proofs and arguments for a decision in his favor, he must appeal to some decision-making guide, which ideally is sufficiently specific to qualify as a rule, principle, or standard. If there were no such narrowly drawn guides, the participation of the litigants would not be meaningful because they would be joining issue in an "intellectual void."[47]

It should be stressed that the adjudicative model we are discussing is an ideal-typical characterization.[48] Reality will frequently fall short of the ideal. Some decisions within an adjudicative framework are no more than *ex post facto* rationalizations of positions formulated in advance. In addition, the symbols surrounding the judicial format may be manipulated to reassure people that the "rules of the game" have been followed, thereby obtaining their "quiescence" in the face of decisions that would otherwise be unacceptable.[49]

Adjudication will thus refer here to the technique of decision making that guarantees participation to parties affected, through a number of procedural devices. The more procedural devices used, the more "judicialized" the process will be. The technique may be the sole forum for the elaboration of policies (as for example in many licence-applications) or it may be a forum where previous administrative determinations are challenged (as for example in welfare appeals). We shall be comparing adjudication as case-by-case elaboration of legislative policy both with administrative decision making by rules determined in advance of specific dispute-situations and with case-by-case discretionary determination that is not controlled by predetermined rules, nor by the adjudicative format.

The Merits of Adjudication

Perhaps the most obvious merits of adjudication for the litigant arise from the fact that it guarantees participation to affected parties. Although they do not make the final decision, the litigants are involved in the decision making process, and are permitted to plead for a decision in their favor and to challenge each other's proofs and arguments. Being immediately involved, they are well placed to advance the strongest case for their proposition. Rules, as we have seen, are in a sense nonrational. Whatever the reasoning behind the enactment of a rule, the rule itself appears as an injunction—for example, not to exceed 55 miles per hour or park 15 feet from a fire hydrant. The adjudicator's obligation to reason will provide a check against the use of criteria that are improper, arbitrary, or legalistic, or fail to achieve congruence between the effect of the decision and official objectives. Adjudication contains a desire to give "formal and institutional expression to the influence of reasoned argument in human affairs."[50] The requirement that a decision be justified, and the justification be published, implies that the justification is open to public criticism. Thus adjudication normally provides an opportunity for scrunity and thus for the accountability of the decision makers to their clientele and to the public.

What strengthens this point is the *nature* of the justifications embodied in judicial decisions. Such decisions must be justified by a rule, standard, or principle. Ascriptive or particularistic criteria are illegitimate. Litigants will make their claims as members of a generalized category. In consequence, an appeal to power, private interests, or political expediency will be inappropriate. The adjudicator will in turn be bound to evaluate the claims by means of accepted techniques and by reference to authoritative guides, rather than his personal interest in the result or his personal predisposition towards the claimants.

A rule might provide administrators with a welcome refuge from the obligation of reasoned decision and from political and personal pressures. Adjudication, on the other hand, might require a reasoned decision. However, the claimant's appeal to a rule, principle, or standard reduces the possibility of litigants' appealing to political or private interests. In this sense, therefore, the decision maker will be somewhat insulated from such pressures.

Administrators might also derive benefits from the fact that a reasoned decision was made and openly arrived at with equal participation. The process of adjudication, whatever the decision, might therefore provide administrative action with the gloss of legitimacy.

A final merit of adjudication is the fact that it involves incremental elaboration of laws on a case-by-case basis. Although an organization might feel itself bound by its own decisions, adjudication deals with a specific fact situation, and later cases can be "distinguished" from earlier ones on the basis of the facts. Thus, despite pressures for consistency, which might lead to a rule's ossification, and for the gradual reduction of discretion (features that students of the common law know too well), the case-by-case approach of adjudication allows an administrative body to deal with cases as they arise and to build its commitments gradually, and even to change its mind.

The Defects of Adjudication

The opportunity to challenge an administrative decision through adjudication does not speak to the nature of the substantive right in question. A welfare recipient, for example, who has the procedural right to appeal the decision of a caseworker, might be told by the appeals referee that what she is asserting does not exist. In other words, she may be told through the exercise of her procedural right that in fact she has no substantive right.[51]

We should also repeat what was stated in connection with rules: The existence of rule-determined (or, in this case, adjudication-determined) rights or obligations does not reflect upon the content of the right or obligation. For example, a welfare "right" to a given amount per month does not imply that the right will be generous or fair, or even that it will be more generous or more fair than a "privilege" given through an official's discretion. The existence of a right *qua* right simply informs us of two factors: that the official's discretion to act is limited and that all persons equally situated ought to receive equal treatment in connection with the right. Moreover, the adversary structure of adjudication might contain costs. In welfare cases, we shall see that the continuing relationship between the caseworker and recipient might make a recipient reluctant to risk antagonizing her caseworker through challenge in an adversary situation. Tenants might fear that a legal challenge to their landlord would provoke retaliation. Adversary challenge in a university setting might prove threatening to the pursuit of learning.[52]

The adversary-adjudicative situation also places the participants in what game theorists call a "zero-sum" situation. One side must win; the other must lose. The defendant is liable or not liable, guilty or not guilty. Except for the possibility of a flexible settlement out of court, the matter is placed in a clear yes-no, either-or, more-or-less setting. Matters that are suited to compromise, mediation, and accommodation are not best pursued in the structured adversary setting of adjudication.[53]

Rules, as we have seen, may be of benefit to officials as a means of announcing policies to affected parties. Individual application of laws is thus possible without the necessity of administrative intervention. Adjudicative decisions, however, are less possible of communication because they arise in the context of specific dispute-situations. In addition, the adjudicative decision is less available to the lay public. Even lawyers may have difficulty in extrapolating the *ratio* from a decision and in knowing the precise content of a rule.[54]

The specific dispute orientation of adjudication highlights another defect from the administrative perspective: it concerns individual rights and may thus bear little relation to the primary administrative function, which involves the performance of a particular task. A particular case, for example, may raise questions wider than the question at issue. The adjudicator may deal with the wider questions but is not required to do so, and remarks made on the wider issue are considered strictly *obiter dicta* and thus not binding on future cases. Furthermore, although the specific decision may affect outside parties, the decision maker is not required to consult or to notify these wider interests. For example, a welfare recipient may complain to a referee that she was refused a winter coat by her caseworker. The grant of the coat is of interest to other recipients and to welfare rights organizations. The referee, however, would not normally consult or notify the other recipients or organization and would confine his decision to the particular recipient at hand.

These defects of adjudication point up its limitations as a planning device. In fact, decision makers in the adjudicative context may lay their own complaints, announce their rules clearly, deal with issues wider than the question at issue,[55] and consult interests wider than those directly represented by the litigants.[56] Normally, however, adjudication is deficient in wide-range planning because it is geared to the resolution of individual disputes rather than to the managerial tasks required to "get the work of society done."[57]

Summary of Merits and Defects

What conclusions can we draw from the checklist of merits and defects of rules and adjudication? The answer is surely none, other than that as methods of controlling administrative discretion each possesses both costs and benefits to the bureaucrat, affected persons, and public. What is gained in uniformity may be lost in flexibility; rules to prevent the arbitrary may encourage the legalistic; case-by-case adjudication may prevent comprehensive planning; rules that may shield the bureaucrat from pressures and allow the efficient and speedy dispatch of cases, may offend the client who desires individually tailored justice.

It is thus clearly futile to propose legal control of administrative discretion in the abstract, for in the abstract the relative merits of devices of legal control may seem evenly balanced by their defects. In assessing whether any given administrative task ought to be subjected to legal control, it is necessary first to recognize that costs and benefits exist and then to weigh one against the other.

Following chapters will attempt to discover more precise criteria by which to assess the suitability of a task to legal control by distinguishing the nature of the task to be performed. First, however, we should consider a major problem facing both law and bureaucracy: the problem of access.

ACCESS TO LAW AND BUREAUCRACY

Laws command obedience. If they are not obeyed, they can be enforced; but their enforcement is not automatically triggered, for the legal process is rarely self-initiating. A rule does not "itself step forward to claim its own instances."[58] Someone has to take action in order to assert a right or enforce an obligation. When A hits B over the head, A might well forget about it, unless B or a law-enforcement officer has the time, opportunity, capacity, or inclination to initiate legal response.

Controlling official discretion through law relies on aggrieved individuals themselves taking action. However, the proponents of legal constraints too often ignore the fact that the initiation of legal action may contain costs for its intended beneficiaries and that access to law and to bureaucracy is frequently limited.

Obviously "full" utilization of the opportunity of access cannot be expected, and may even render organizational ends ineffective.[59] Because most bureaucracies are constrained by limited resources, limited manpower, and limited time, too high a level of access could preclude satisfactory attention to individual cases or to the broader purposes that the bureaucracy is charged with achieving. Impeded access to bureaucracy must, however, raise concern where the obstacles to access are unevenly distributed. And where the obstacles affect some social groups more than others, the concern, by standards of social justice, might prove the more acute.

Literature on the subject (rarely from legal sources) does indicate that some groups may possess special problems about relations with bureaucracy. For example, in describing the inhabitants of the Italian section of Boston known as the West End, Herbert Gans explains their difficulty in dealing with government bureaucracy as being due to their inability to recognize the existence of "object oriented" organization, governed by other than "peer group" rules.[60] Gans found that the idea that individual officials follow rules and regulations based not on personal morality but on concepts of efficiency, order, administrative heirarchy, and the like is, for the West Enders, difficult to accept.

Attitudes revealed in the present study often showed similarities to those described by Gans, with people unwilling to pursue their rights through "object-oriented" rules. For example, a welfare recipient refused to sign a form verifying his unemployment and appealed to the referee to "take my word for it as a man." Others refused to sign forms certifying illness, as a precondition to the grant of a telephone, or refused to report the theft of a check to the police. One welfare recipient refused to fulfill the requirement of obtaining estimates from three stores as a precondition to obtaining a new crib. This recipient bought a secondhand crib from a neighbor and could not understand why she was not reimbursed for the item, which was cheaper by far than a new crib. The assertion of legal rights, however, very often requires formal procedures.

Gans' study also describes the interrelations between the citizens of the area and the "public caretakers" (institutions, including welfare organizations, and individuals offering care to residents of the area). Gans reveals that a vast "cultural barrier" prevented the satisfactory interaction between the West Enders and these caretakers. The caretakers feared and disapproved of the people of the area and presented them with a "middle-class value pattern . . . not only in programs, but in the recruitment and training of professions in the creation of a professional image and self-image, and, most important, in the structure of professional-client relationships."[61] The West Enders in turn reacted to the caretakers with a mood of "sullen hostility,"[62] preferring to obtain at least some of the help they required from their own "internal caretakers," that is, neighbors, peers, store owners, and even bartenders. Apart from their conception of the caretakers as a group, the West Enders were "convinced that the police, the government bureaucracy, the elected officials and the courts are corrupt and are engaged in a never ending conspiracy to deprive the citizens of what is morally theirs."[63] The West Enders therefore "play it safe" by minimizing relationships with the bureaucracy.

The present study revealed similar attitudes on the part of the residents of the Madison Park area. Over one-half of those interviewed agreed with statements such as "I don't think public officials care what people like me think,"[64] "People like me don't have any say about what government does,"[65] and "There's no way a person like me can change what government officials do."[66] A significantly higher percentage of the low-education population agreed with the statements in each case.[67] Of the Madison Park residents and welfare appellants interviewed, over half claimed that social workers could not understand people in their situation.[68] A significantly higher proportion of the black respondents felt this way.[69]

To whatever extent we may generalize from these responses, they are suggestive, together with Gans' description, that many people of low educational status and low income are likely to estimate that they will receive unsympathetic responses from bureaucracy. Whether this assessment is caused by cultural factors or is a factor of "lower-class" value patterns,[70] "powerlessness" or "alienation" does not for our present purposes require an answer. The accuracy of the predictions will be tested below, although this will not affect any function they may have in actually deterring access to bureaucracy.[71]   The fact, however, that these and other factors inhibit the utilization of rights or the enforcement of obligations through bureaucracy should, if they exist, be recognized and acknowledged as a crucial factor in the debate concerning bureaucracy's legalization or judicialization.

The following three chapters will consider the question of access by examining three situations that attempt to highlight the problem in different ways and to specify as precisely as possible, through case studies of the agencies and consideration of the attitudes of their clientele, where obstacles to access may lie. Later chapters will discuss the extent to which obstacles revealed may be removed.

Notes

1. L. Fuller, *The Morality of Law*, at 106 (1959).

2. "With legalization, policies are transformed into rules that bind the decider" [P. Nonet, *Administrative Justice*, at 246 (1969)]. A more detailed discussion of the distinctions between policies, principles, rules, and standards will be undertaken in Chapter 5, in the discussion of the functional limits of rules.

3. K. C. Davis, *Discretionary Justice, A Preliminary Inquiry*, at 65 (1969).

4. *Ibid.*, at 30. This view is propounded by writers such as J. Dickinson, *Administrative Justice and the Supremacy of Law* (1927), and F. Hayeck, *The Road to Serfdom* (1944).

5. See Fuller's requirements for "the morality that makes law possible," *op. cit.*, esp. pp. 44-94.

6. On this point, see generally L. Friedman, "Legal Rules and the Process of Social Change," 19 *Stan. L. Rev.* 786, 792 (1967).

7. Si Santo v. Commonwealth of Pennsylvania, 273 U.S. 34, 42, 47, S.Ct. 267, 270, 71 L. Ed. 524 (1927).

8. See Fuller, *op. cit.*, at 81, who refers to the "Congruence between Official Action and Declared Rule." As will be suggested later, official policy may not specifically be declared.

The Legal Control of Bureaucracy

9. Selznick defines "legality" as "a set of standards . . . [which] seeks progressively to reduce the degree of arbitrariness in positive law and administration" [P. Selznick, *Law, Society and Industrial Justice*, at 12 (1969)].

10. R. Pound, *Jurisprudence*, vol. 2, at 383 (1959).

11. For an example of the changing function of public housing, from a program initially to provide for the "submerged middle class," and later for the lower class, see L. Friedman, "Public Housing and the Poor: An Overview," 54 *Calif. L. Rev.* 642 (1966).

12. In Chapter 6.

13. A by-product of this would be to achieve uniformity of application, as considered above. Davis considers that "the chief hope for confining discretionary power does not lie in statutory enactments but in much more extensive administrative rule-making" (*op. cit.*, at 55).

14. Pound lists six advantages of the "administration of justice according to law," one of which is that law secures against "improper motives" on the part of those who administer justice (*op. cit.*, at 381).

15. On selective enforcement by the police, see generally, La Fave, *Arrest: The Decision to Take a Suspect into Custody* (1965); J. Q. Wilson, *Varieties of Police Behavior* (1968); J. Skolnick, *Justice Without Trial* (1966).

16. Thus Selznick's definition of arbitrary rules cannot be accepted: "Rules are arbitrary when they reflect confused policies, are based on ignorance or error, and when they suggest no inherent principles of criticism" (*op. cit.*, at 13). Selznick's definition of arbitrary discretion would, however, be closer to the definition here: "Discretion is arbitrary when it is whimsical, or governed by criteria extraneous to legitimate means or ends" (*ibid.*).

17. J. Shklar defines legalism as an "ethical attitude that holds moral conduct to be a matter of rule-following . . ." [*Legalism*, at 1 (1964)].

18. For a discussion of these cases see Friedman, *op. cit.*, note 11, pp. 654-661. See also Davis, *op. cit.*, pp. 77-80.

19. This question as it relates to welfare "rights" will be considered in Chapter 5.

20. P. Nonet, *Administrative Justice*, at 6 (1969).

21. *Ibid.*, at 251.

22. *Ibid.*, at 170.

23. P. Selznick, *Law, Society and Industrial Justice* (1969).

24. Defined by Selznick as the concern for "reducing the arbitrariness of official action and for reconceiving the rights of students and faculty" (*ibid.* at 28-29). For Selznick's definition of "arbitrary," see note 16, above.

25. *Ibid.*, at 29.

26. *Ibid.*, at 30.

27. See, e.g., D. Shapiro, "The Choice of Rulemaking and Adjudication in the Development of Administrative Policy," 78 *Harv. L. Rev.*

921 (1965); H. Friendly, *The Federal Administrative Agencies: The Need for a Better Definition of Standards* (1962); Davis, *op. cit.*

28. This point is qualified by Shapiro, *op. cit.*, at 930-932.

29. 5 U.S.C. s. 553 (Supp. IV, 1969).

30. *Ibid.*, s. 553(b) 3(A).

31. See, generally, A. Bonfield, "Some Tentative Thoughts on Public Participation in the Making of Interpretative Rules and General Statements of Policy Under the A.P.A.," 23 *Admin. L. Rev.* 101 (1971).

32. M. Weber, *The Theory of Social and Economic Organization*, trans. E. Henderson and T. Parsons, at 340 (1947).

33. Selznick, *op. cit.*, at 88, refers to the seniority rule as an objective standard for promotion, reducing management's free choice, but welcomed as "a contribution to orderly management," since it "reflects a need (of management) for objective criteria that can be applied easily, systematically, and with beneficial effects on employee morale."

34. Wilson, *op. cit.*, at 181.

35. *Supra*, p. 17

36. V. Thompson, *Modern Organization*, at 17 (1961).

37. Weber, *op. cit.*, note 32.

38. Murray Edelman [*The Symbolic Uses of Politics* (1967)] refers to the ritual behind enforcement by "petty bureaucrats" of rules: "These are unseen and untouchable and hence, like all dogma, not to be violated, altered or questioned. Their invocation is a signal that discussion of the merits is out of place and profane, and what is invoked is the transmission and conservation of a sacred tradition" (at 112).

39. See Davis, *op. cit.*, at 79.

40. Friedman, *op. cit.*, note 11, at 667-668. See also L. Friedman, "On Legalistic Reasoning—A Footnote to Weber," *Wis. L. Rev.* 148 (1966), where Friedman discusses further the "nonrational" element of legislation: "A law appears normally as naked *fiat*, as plain and uncompromising as the Ten Commandments" (at 159).

41. Friedman, *op. cit.*, note 11, at 661.

42. V. Thompson, *Modern Organization*, chap. 9 (1961). This behavior is seen by Thompson as arising out of specialization, where the party in authority has a need to control those subordinate to himself.

43. *Ibid.*, at 160.

44. Compare the "status dysfunctions" observed by Barnard as arising out of the anxieties of superiors stemming from their awareness of their growing incompetence as specialists. The superiors tend in consequence to require more and more uncritical adherence to established rules, while subordinates hesitate to draw on their expertise to challenge an existing rule, for fear that the challenge would be viewed by their superiors as threatening. C. Barnard, "The Function of Status Systems," in R. Merton, ed., *Reader in Bureaucracy*, at 242 (1952).

45. Reich, "The New Property," 73 *Yale L.J.* 733 (1964).

46. L. Fuller, "Collective Bargaining and the Arbitrator," 1 *Wis. L. Rev.* 3 (1963). See also L. Fuller, "The Forms and Limits of Adjudication" (unpublished paper); H. Hart and A. Sacks, *The Legal Process* (tentative ed., 1958). See generally, P. Weiler, "Two Models of Judicial Decision-Making," *Can B. Rev.* 406 (1968).

47. Fuller, *op. cit.*, at 28.

48. An ideal type "is a freely created neutral construct by means of which an attempt is made to 'order' reality by isolating, accentuating, and articulating the elements of a recurrent social phenomenon . . . into an internally consistent system of relationships." J. Gould and W. K. Kolb, eds., *UNESCO Dictionary of the Social Sciences* (1964) at p. 312. See also E. Shils and H. Finch, *Max Weber on the Methodology of the Social Sciences* at p. 90 (1969). Fuller is clearly suggesting an ideal-typical situation himself. See e.g. Fuller, "Collective Bargaining and the Arbitrator" *Wis. L. Rev.* 34 (1963).

49. M. Edelman, *The Symbolic Uses of Politics* (1964), where this point about "symbolic reassurance" is made.

50. Fuller, *Forms and Limits, op. cit.*, at 13.

51. Thus Davis (*op. cit.*, at 184) is surely wrong in stating that a claimant for public assistance in a federally assisted program has a "right" to welfare, simply because the federal requirements provide for a hearing and judicial review.

52. See Dixon v. Alabama, 294 F. 2d. 150 (1961).

53. This point will be pursued further with regard to "polycentric problems" in Chapter 5.

54. Shapiro, *op. cit.*, at 941, makes the additional point that a lawyer may "rely on some commentator's summary, which may oversimplify, omit, or simply be out of date."

55. See *ibid.*, at 937, on the "distortion" of the adjudicative process.

56. *Ibid.*, at 931, refers to instances where the federal administrative agencies do receive wider comment in the course of adjudicative proceedings.

57. Selznick, *op. cit.*, at 16. Selznick distinguishes adjudication and administration by the fact that the prime function of adjudication is to "realize the ideals of legality" and "discover the legal coordinates of a particular situation." Administration, however, attempts to manipulate a situation to "achieve a desired outcome." Administration and adjudication share a "common commitment to objective and impersonal decision making."

58. H. L. A. Hart, *The Concept of Law*, at 123 (1961).

59. See L. Milbraith, *Political Participation* (1965), for the argument that moderate levels of political participation are desirable.

60. H. Gans, *The Urban Villagers* (1962).

61. *Ibid.*, at 274.

62. *Ibid.*, at 155.

63. *Ibid.*, at 163.

64. Fifty-five percent (55) agreed, 41% (41) disagreed, 4% other responses. "Agree" refers to responses: "strongly agree" and "agree."

65. Fifty-five percent (55) agreed, 44% (44) disagreed, 1% other responses.

66. Fifty-nine percent (59) agreed, 41% (41) disagreed. The first two statements were taken from A. Campbell's "political efficacy" scale [*The Voter Decides* (1954)]. The third statement was designed for the purpose of the present study.

67. For example, the differences between low-education (less than 8 years) and high-education (high school graduates) responses in each case was: Question 1: 67% low education, 38% high education agree; Question 2: 76% low education, 26% high education agree; Question 3: 82% low education, 37% high education agree.

68. Fifty-seven percent (57) agreed, 43% (43) disagreed.

69. Of blacks, 70.6% (41) agreed, 29.4% (17) disagreed. Of whites, 38.1% (16) agreed, 61.9% (26) disagreed. However, race did not influence the responses to the above three questions significantly.

70. See E. Banfield, *The Unheavenly City* (1970).

71. "The propertyless masses especially are not served by a formal 'equality before the law' and a 'calculable' adjudication and administration, as demanded by 'bourgeois' interests. Naturally, in their eyes justice and administration should serve to compensate for their economic and social life-opportunities in the face of the propertied classes." H. Gerth and C. Mills, eds., *From Max Weber*, at 221 (1958).

2

Complaints Against Officials: Welfare Appeals

The last chapter has suggested that a major limit to the value of legal controls over bureaucracy in general, and of legal remedies enforceable through bureaucracy in particular, is the failure of many persons to utilize the rights they may have. It has been hypothesized that the problem of access might prove a major obstacle to the utilization of rights, particularly in the case of the poor or poorly educated.

The following three chapters attempt to test this hypothesis and to locate the nature and extent of obstacles to access to bureaucracy in the context of three different situations. This chapter will consider the situation in which a person affected by an administrative ruling appeals that ruling to appropriate officials. Our example will be a welfare applicant or recipient who appeals to a referee to overturn a caseworker's decision. The setting is a district office of the Boston Department of Welfare. Seventy appeals within a one-year period were attended by the author, the case files of each appellant were read, and 42 of the appellants were interviewed formally by professional interviewers.[1]

Before examining the appeal system in operation, we must review the organizational structure of welfare in Boston.

ORGANIZATIONAL STRUCTURE AND PROCEDURES

From the seventeenth century, New England followed the

pattern of the English Poor Law under which each town was responsible for its own poor.[2] The town officials, known as "selectmen," were initially charged with the task of providing for the poor. Their task, however, soon became "so burdensome as to hamper the usual machinery of town government,"[3] mainly because the case of each pauper was debated on its merits at a town meeting. As a result, Boston became the first town in America to bureaucratize the task of providing for the poor, creating in 1691 a separate body known as "overseers of the poor." The first instance of state assistance to the poor occurred in 1675, when the Massachusetts Provincial Treasury was authorized to reimburse towns that had to support a large influx of refugees during the war with the Indians.[4] This act set the pattern for later years, and up until 1935 the administration of public assistance was almost entirely carried out at the local level, with the state providing supervision and financial aid.[5]

In 1935, on the day Congress passed the Social Security Act, part of President Roosevelt's "New Deal package,"[6] the Massachusetts legislature passed legislation which empowered the state to accept the federal funds that were to become available in the form of grants-in-aid.[7] The federal law allows states to take advantage of the grants for the benefit of the categories of dependent person described.[8] The Department of Health, Education, and Welfare, responsible for the law's administration, has preferred to define standards for receiving the grants in terms of relatively flexible "principles" instead of detailed methods and practices,[9] and has largely confined its own functions to consultation, budget estimates and reviews, fiscal audits, and enforcement of personnel standards.[10]

Eligibility Criteria

At the time of this study the State Department of Public Welfare issued the rules and regulations determining the standards of public assistance in Massachusetts. The introduction to the looseleaf *Massachusetts Public Assistance Manual*[11] states that

All residents of Massachusetts have a right to apply for public assistance and to receive financial assistance and social services whenever they are needed.

Need is defined as

a condition resulting from lack of income or other resources sufficient to maintain a content of living compatible with health, decency and self respect. [12]

The statutes and the manual together spell out the detailed requirements for eligibility under five separate programs:

1. To be eligible for Old Age Assistance (OAA), an applicant must be at least 65 years of age, have resided in the Commonwealth for at least one year immediately preceding the application, and be the owner of personal property of not more than $500.

2. To be eligible for Medical Aid for the Aged (MAA), an applicant must be at least sixty-five years of age and a resident of the state (of no particular duration). He may own personal property of up to $2000.[13]

3. A Disability Assistance (DA) recipient must be between the ages of eighteen and sixty-five, a resident of the Commonwealth for at least one year preceding the application, the owner of not more than $500 worth of personal property, and "permanently and totally disabled." In accordance with federal requirements this condition is not equivalent to "complete helplessness" but is limited to persons whose "Physical and mental condition is such that there is no reasonable likelihood that the person can attain a condition of self-support (or, in the case of a homemaker, the capacity to maintain a household) except through medical treatment, physical restoration, vocational training and rehabilitation."[14]

4. To be eligible for Aid to Families with Dependent Children (AFDC), an applicant must be the parent[15] or "grantee relative" of a child under eighteen years of age (twenty-one if in an educational institution) who has been "deprived of parental support due to the death, physical or mental incapacity, unemployment or continued absence from the home of either parent."[16] The child must have been residing in the Commonwealth for at least one year prior to the application and must be living in the home of the parent or grantee relative. The child and his mother and father may not own combined personal property worth more than $300.

5. General Relief is a residual category, with no residence requirement. The act merely emphasizes the traditional by stating that "Every town shall relieve and support all poor and indigent persons residing or found therein whenever they stand in need thereof."[17]

Chapter IV of the manual contains 42 pages of complex rules[18] for the determination of "budgetary needs" and the standards for evaluating income. The "Basic Budgetary Needs"[19] are calculated according to a strict scale and determined according to the number of persons participating in the grant, the number and age of the children, and whether household expenses are to be shared. To give an example of the standards: A woman supporting three children aged ten, eight, and four would be given $246 per month on AFDC.[20]

The manual also makes provision for assistance to cover "nonrecurring needs" (such as moving and storage expenses), and "nonbasic needs," which include medical assistance, and "special needs," which means "nursing or housekeeping services and other special needs as laundry, household chores, telephone, special diet, etc., as required on a casework basis."[21]

The Organizational Setting

At the time of this study, from March 1967 to March 1968, the Boston Department of Public Welfare was one of the 220 local welfare boards in Massachusetts.[22] The average caseload for the city was 40,000, at a total cost of $8 million.[23] The processing of the cases was carried out by six district offices. This study will focus on the operations of one of these.

The area serviced by the district office is estimated to consist of a population of c. 100,000, approximately half of whom are estimated to be black. The caseload averaged 9500, about one in five of the total Boston average.[24] During the year, 6000 new applications (including reapplications) were processed, of which about 14 percent were denied.[25]

The office is presided over by the head social work supervisor with two principal social work supervisors next in line. Three adult units, dealing with unattached family cases (largely OAA, MAA, and DA), are each headed by a social work supervisor under whom work six or seven social caseworkers, with two clerical workers to a unit. Each unit deals with a particular area. Seven family units (dealing largely with AFDC cases) are organized in a similar way. In addition, two social workers are available for intake where new applications are processed.

A person applying for assistance must appear at the intake section and supply information by which his eligibility may be determined. If the application is urgent, the person will normally be placed on general relief pending a home visit by the social worker assigned to the case. A visit to an applicant's home will be routinely undertaken in order to assess the home environment and the validity of the claim of eligibility.[26]

A person granted assistance will be sent a check covering his grant twice a month. The social worker will conduct home visits once every three months for clients on AFDC, DA, and OAA, and once every six months for clients receiving general relief.[27] Approval of a request for a grant covering a special need will be determined at the discretion of the social worker. A request for a special need in excess of $100 is customarily referred to the head social work supervisor.

An applicant who is refused aid and a recipient whose aid is suspended, terminated, or altered will be informed of his right to a "fair hearing." Those receiving or applying for OAA will be sent an appeal blank; others will be informed of their right to request one.[28] The hearing will then take place at the district office where a referee appointed by the State Board of Welfare would appear. Where the hearing takes the form of a review the appellant would not appear, but at an appeal the appellant would present his own case, unless he was represented by a lawyer or a welfare rights organization such as the Mothers for Adequate Welfare (MAWS). The caseworker (or her supervisor) would appear to defend her ruling.

Although a legal remedy is provided to an aggrieved recipient or applicant, it should be noted that the remedy is not self-initiating. The appellant will himself have to initiate a complaint. However, three main factors might inhibit the utilization of the appeal proceedings: first, a lack of knowledge of the law; second, a lack of knowledge of the appeal procedures; and third, an assessment that the costs involved in appealing might not make the probable benefits worth striving for. These potential obstacles will be considered in turn—after we attempt to assess to what extent aggrieved recipients or applicants made use of the appeals procedure.

WELFARE APPEALS IN BOSTON, MARCH 1967-1968

Seventy appeals were laid[29] at the district office out of a caseload for the year of 9500.[30] Although this figure might at first glance appear small, we have no way of verifying this fact without knowledge of how many applicants or recipients felt wronged by a caseworker's decision. Although we know that seven out of ten appeals were laid by current recipients appealing the sufficiency of their grant,[31] we do not know what percentage of dissatisfied recipients these appellants represent. A somewhat clearer idea of the proportion of dissatisfied applicants or recipients who appeal might be gained by examining the number of appeals against denials of applications for welfare and against the withdrawal of assistance. During the one-year period the district office processed just over 6000 new applications for assistance of which 829 (13.5 percent) were denied.[32] By no means were all of the denied applications appealable. Decisions concerning general relief, as we have seen, are not appealable. In addition, tabulations giving the reasons for appeals being rejected in Boston[33] show that a consistent 40 percent of all denied applications were turned down for what might be termed nonappealable reasons such as death,[34] voluntary withdrawals, or failure to contact the office.[35] The appealable denials constituted approximately 60 percent of all categories and excluded general relief.

The tabulations in Table 2.1 below show that none of the 50 AFDC applicants denied assistance appealed,[36] and only 2.8 percent of the total, or approximately 1 out of 35 applicants[37] denied assistance on appealable grounds, actually lodged an appeal.

Table 2.1 Appeals Against Denied Welfare Applications, by Category, District Office, March 1967-March 1969

Category	OAA	MA	AFDC	DA	GR	Total
Total applications denied	65	523	83	84	63	829
Appealable denials (est. 60% of total denied)	39	314	50	50	0	460
Appeals against denials	2	4	0	7	—	13
Percentage of appeals of appealable denials	5.1	1.2	0.0	14.0	—	2.8

During the period of this study, 22.6 percent of the total caseload at the district office (2160 of the total caseload of 9550) was withdrawn. General relief cases showed a particularly high turnover rate.[38] Again, however, it should be borne in mind that not all the cases withdrawn may be appealed. General relief cases constitute the first exception. Other cases were withdrawn because of the death of the recipient[39] or the failure of the recipient to request further aid or to be contacted.[40]

Table 2.2 shows that only 1.5 percent, or about 1 out of every 70 recipients whose assistance was withdrawn for a reason that was appealable, actually lodged an appeal.[41]

Table 2.2   Appeals Against Withdrawn Welfare Cases, by Category, District Office, March 1967-March 1968

Category	OAA	MA	AFDC	DA	GR	Total
Total withdrawals	360	360	528	144	768	2160
Appealable withdrawals*	86	86	300	66	0	538
Appeals against withdrawals	1	0	5	2	–	8
Percentage of appeals of appealable withdrawals	0.9	0.0	1.7	3.0	–	1.5

*Based on percentage of appealable withdrawals in Boston for the same period: OAA and MA, 24%; AFDC, 57%; DA, 46%; and total, 39%.

To sum up, we have seen that 1 in 190 recipients complained about the sufficiency of their budget during the course of one year.[42] Only 1 out of 35 appeals resulted from applications for welfare that were denied and appealable. No AFDC applicant appealed such a denial. Of the recipients whose welfare assistance was withdrawn for reasons appealable, only 1 in 70 appealed.

Although we cannot be sure how many applicants or recipients were dissatisfied with a caseworker's decision, it would probably not be too speculative to assume from these figures that very few potential appellants utilize the appeals procedure. This assumption is supported by other evidence. Thirty-two randomly selected welfare recipients in the Madison Park area were asked whether they had been unhappy with a caseworker's decision. Thirteen claimed to have been dissatisfied. Of these, however, only one had actually laid an appeal to redress his grievance.[43]

Despite the small sample and speculative interpretation here, it is submitted that, taken together, and combined with Handler's surveys,[44] we have sufficient evidence to show that a very small proportion of aggrieved recipients or applicants utilize the appeal procedures. We shall now examine why this might be so.

OBSTACLES TO THE INITIATION OF WELFARE APPEALS

Knowledge of the Law

Before a person will lodge an appeal, he must feel legally wronged. This point seems obvious, but it would be difficult for an applicant or recipient to be aware of any rights that he has. At the time of this study, access to knowledge of the law was limited. Few recipients would know about the existence of the policy manual. In order to study it, the recipient would have to come into the district office and read it there. In one case an appellant asked to see the relevant rule. The caseworker agreed to send her a copy, although it was "not customary" to do this. The manual itself is a large volume outlining complicated budgetary calculations. Few recipients would begin to comprehend it.

Knowledge of any legal remedy would therefore seem in practice to be limited to recipients with personal knowledge of the system, to those who are in touch with a welfare rights organization such as the Mothers for Adequate Welfare, or to those who have access to a knowledgeable lawyer. Even so, however, a recipient's personal knowledge of a past decision—relating to her own case or to that of another—would not necessarily lead to the conclusion that the decision would be followed, unless a clear rule specified that it would be. Hearing referees are adamant that they are under no obligation to follow precedent. One referee specifically told an appellant at a hearing, "I don't give a damn if I find myself at odds with decisions of other referees. I don't care what happened yesterday." Because case records are confidential, neither a recipient nor a lawyer is able to compare the decisions reached in other cases. In one case an appellant's lawyer requested access to her case record prior to the hearing. This was the first time that the district office had received such a request. The decision was made to allow the lawyer access to "releases"—that is, any material issued by the department to the recipient, such as notification of amounts of assistance. Access was not given, however, to the written summaries and reports of the caseworkers, which reveal much more about the reasons behind the official decisions.[45]

Apart from the mechanical difficulties of knowing the law, other factors may account for a welfare recipient's not knowing he may appeal a decision. For example, recipients often do not understand complicated assessments of their budgets. Most people who receive professional services must surrender to professional authority. Few patients can challenge the dentist's interpretation of a tooth X-ray. The welfare caseworker's calculations and pronouncement may seem just as immune to challenge. An illustration of the way in which the budget is calculated shows why.

When a person first applies for welfare, he goes to the intake section of his local district office where a caseworker will help him fill out a form requesting information about the extent of his financial resources, both capital and income.

Whether a person is considered eligible for a welfare grant will then depend upon whether the value of these resources is below a certain figure. This figure (e.g., $240 per month income for a mother living alone with three children and with total capital resources of less than $2000) is considered the cutoff point for eligibility for the category of person involved, and the mother will receive as a grant the amount by which this eligibility standard—known in Massachusetts as "basic budgetary need"—exceeds her available monthly resources. For example, if she has no capital and her present income is $100 per month, she will be eligible for a grant of $140, to make up the "basic budgetary need" of $240 for a person in her category. Once eligibility has been allowed, it is reviewed on a regular and continuing basis, in order to determine whether changing circumstances such as a lump-sum insurance payment or the birth of another child have caused her income or category to change, thus requiring an alteration in her budget or the termination of aid.

We see, therefore, that the budgetary calculation is, and appears to be, complex. The recipient's condition changes, thus involving budgetary changes. Were the caseworker to make an error in calculating the budget, the recipient would be subject to these errors and unlikely to know how to get them rectified. For example, two recipients initiated appeals only when their budgets were suddenly altered in order to rectify a caseworker error. During the course of five appeal hearings, a basic error in the budgetary calculation—to the detriment of the recipient—was discovered. The recipient is dependent for necessities upon her caseworker's budgetary calculation—and subject to the caseworker's competence.

The theoretical justification of a cash payment rather than a payment in kind is in part that it provides the recipient with free choice in spending her grant.[46] Those who would separate the caseworker's income-maintenance function (administration of a client's budget) from the "rehabilitative" or "social service" function[47] seem to assume that budgetary administration involves no discretion or powers of coercion over the recipient. In practice, however, the caseworker's determination of the client's budget involves discretion, which gives the caseworker a degree of control over the client's resources and therefore restricts the client's freedom to spend on items of her choice.

The first reason for this is that the budget figures are low and do not seem to allow for commodities and activities[48] that middle-class people routinely enjoy—for example, alcohol or television sets. Nor is there much room for emergencies. The recipient thus frequently exhausts her funds before the date of her next grant and needs a special grant to tide her over. The caseworker decides whether a special grant will be given.

In addition, budgetary determination itself involves an element of discretion on the caseworker's part. For example, at the time of this study, the objective eligibility standard for a mother with three children was available resources of $240 per month income and capital of less than $2000. At the hour of application the mother might have an income of $100 and capital of $1000. The value of these resources would seem objectively to qualify her for aid, assuming the truth of her statement. But the calculation is not that simple, as the following cases show.

Mrs. A. had received an insurance payment of $3000 one month prior to her application, most of which she had spent in the interval. The caseworker refused aid on the ground that the recently received insurance monies should have provided for her needs, even though the worker admitted that the money had been "dissipated" on items such as graduation expenses for her daughter and badly needed repairs to her television set and washing machine. This decision was reversed on appeal.

Mrs. B., a woman who had been receiving welfare for some time, disclosed in an interview with her caseworker that two weeks before she had received a lump-sum Social Security payment (due to her by virtue of her husband's death) of $1120, most of which had already been spent. The caseworker suspended her grant despite the fact that the money had been spent. On appeal, Mrs. B. explained that she had spent the money on "bedspreads, sheets, and what I needed and welfare doesn't give." The referee, however, agreed with the caseworker's determination that these expenditures were not appropriate and upheld the suspension of aid.

Mrs. R., a divorcee living alone with her two children, applied for welfare, claiming that although she received an income that would be too high to make her eligible for welfare assistance, her available resources were, in fact, below the eligibility maximum because she paid a babysitter to look after her children while she attended classes at a nursing college. The caseworker refused to sanction this as a legitimate expense because it entailed the client's prolonged absence from her home, which, the worker maintained, was not conducive to good child care, and was a "luxury." The appeal referee concurred in the decision to refuse assistance.

These cases indicate how the caseworker's discretion to determine the appropriateness of a recipient's expenditures involves a power to make value judgments about the recipient's behavior and to condition the amount (if any) of welfare assistance upon those expenditures that make such behavior possible.

The need for such discretion can be understood insofar as the welfare agency's obligation to guard the public purse extends. But frequently the control can be exercised in a paternal way, influenced by the philosophy that welfare is a charity, not individually earned, and that those who administer it should see to it that it is not spent, to quote an early spokesman of this philosophy, "on items covered by the phrase 'wine, women and song.' "[49]

The picture of the welfare relationship that is emerging shows a high degree of surrender to professional authority on the part of the recipient, who is dependent upon the benevolent exercise of discretion for the basic necessities of life. Observation of the system shows too that it is misleading to view the caseworker's budget-determination function as simply routine.

In fact, therefore, the recipient is dependent to a large extent on her caseworker's competence (and good faith) and subject to the value judgment involved in the decision about what constitutes an "available resource." The recipient will otherwise be free to spend on items of her own choosing.

As has been suggested, the perception of the situation differs from the facts of the situation. Welfare recipients were asked to evaluate this statement: "Being on welfare means that you have extra money to spend in any way you want." Over 80 percent (62 of 71 interviewed) disagreed. Allowing for some exaggeration in estimating freedom to spend, the recipient's perception of that situation was at variance with the legal facts.

Thirty-eight percent of the recipients (24 of 62) thought that the caseworker had the right to know how a recipient spent her money. Legally the caseworker does not possess such a right. The fact that caseworkers often request much information may account for the relatively high percentage of recipients who believe otherwise. And, in view of the dependent relationship, many recipients might be unwilling even to consider resisting any informal pressures to supply it.

This distinction—between the strictly legal situation, the situation in practice, and the perception of the situation by a potential beneficiary of rights—is one that should be drawn. To give "rights" (e.g., the "right" to welfare) in a context where the "right" will not be recognized, or, if recognized, not exercised, is surely not enough. For example, despite the explicit statement in the *Massachusetts Welfare Manual* that a "right" to welfare exists, only 59 percent of welfare recipients thought that welfare was a right for a person whose income was low enough to qualify. (See Table 2.3.) Forty percent therefore wrongly thought that there was no such right or were ignorant of a right.

Table 2.3 Welfare Recipients' Response to:
*"Would you say that the law gives a right to welfare
assistance to anyone whose income is low enough?*

Response	Percentage	N
Yes	59.2%	42
No	22.5	16
Don't know	18.3	13
Total	100.0	71

Lack of knowledge of the legal situation is also reflected in the recipient's view of her right of privacy. Caseworkers are required to visit a recipient's home regularly (every three months for AFDC recipients) to check eligibility and to continue the "social study" of the recipient's situation. Allegations of invasion of privacy stem primarily from unannounced home visits conducted at night—"midnight raids."[50] The object of these raids is to discover a "man in the house" with whom a woman receiving AFDC might be said to be conducting a "stable relationship." The man would then be considered responsible for supporting the woman's children, and the woman's grant would be terminated.[51]

At the time of this study, midnight raids were not conducted routinely in Massachusetts. If they were conducted in cases of suspected fraud, the author was unaware of them. The welfare manual states that

The individual's privacy and personal dignity are not to be violated in any way. For example, social work staff are not to enter a home by force, without permission, or under false pretenses; make unnecessary home visits outside of working hours, and particularly during sleeping hours, or conduct searches in the home to seek clues to possible deception.[52]

Here too the welfare recipients were not aware of the strictly legal situation. One-third (23 of 71) believed "if someone is on welfare, a social worker has the right to enter his or her home at any time" to be true. Other surveys have reported similar findings.[53] Again we may speculate that this may be true because the recipient has no opportunity to know or because of a suppliant attitude (a feeling that a welfare recipient ought to be grateful and grant a reciprocal right of entry to the caseworker).

The cases studied support the evidence that recipients were frequently unaware of their rights—particularly with regard to budgetary calculations. In two instances appeals were precipitated by the correction of caseworker errors that had stood undisturbed for some months. The fact that the amount of their grants was suddenly changed prompted the recipients to challenge the revised calculations. The incorrect calculation in itself, however, was insufficient to trigger a complaint. In five other cases evidence at the appeal hearing on nonrelated matters inadvertently revealed errors in budgetary calculation that had been standing—to the detriment of the recipient—for some time. The case records revealed several instances where the recipient was unaware of goods or services to which she would have been entitled—for example, orthopedic shoes for a child, special diets, or certain clothing grants. During the course of this study the Mothers for Adequate Welfare organized to inform recipients of some of these rights and supported many of the appeals for special grants. However, little effort to provide such information was made by the Department of Welfare.

Knowledge of the Appeals Procedure

The recipient or applicant who knows that he has been legally wronged will then have to know the appeal procedures. At the time of this study all applicants who were denied assistance were simultaneously informed of their right of appeal. Recipients whose aid was suspended or terminated would be similarly informed. Old Age Assistance applicants or recipients would automatically be sent a blank appeal form; others would be told of their right to receive one on request.

The right to appeal does not extend to applicants or recipients of general relief. However, an applicant for categorical assistance is normally supported through general relief pending verification of his application. Frequently he continues to be supported by general relief when his application for categorical assistance is denied. Unless he appeals this denial immediately (an unlikely event since he does not normally know the technical source of his continued support), he has no right of appeal from any further alteration or termination of his aid, since no appeal lies from assistance through general relief.

In practice, therefore, those who are informed of their appeal rights are applicants not supported through general relief, and recipients whose aid has been suspended or terminated. In all other cases involving a potential appeal, including the denial of special grants and alteration in budget, the recipients are not informed of their rights to appeal.

Thirty-one welfare recipients in Madison Park were asked whether there was anything a person could do to challenge a caseworker's decision. Table 2.4 tabulates the results. Almost half (14) thought there was nothing to be done, and only 4 of the 17 mentioned the appeal procedure as a possibility. Less than 1 in 7 of those interviewed knew about the appeals procedure.[54]

Table 2.4 Welfare Recipients' Knowledge of Appeal Procedures:

"Can you tell me whether there is anything a person can do if he or she wants to get the decision of a welfare worker changed?"

	Percentage	N
Yes		
(a) Approach outside organization	9.7%	3
(b) Persist within department	32.3	10
(c) Appeal	12.9	4
No	45.1	14
Total	100.0%	31

The Willingness to Appeal

Any legal or administrative process that depends for its initiation upon individual action will only be initiated if the individual feels first, that his prospects of benefiting from the process are real, and second, that the costs involved in utilizing the process will be outweighed by the probable benefits so as to make his investment in the process worthwhile. In other words, he must feel that he will probably win his case and that his victory is worth fighting for. It is important to remember that the recipient's assessment of his chances of winning may or may not accord with these chances *in fact*. The recipient's chances of winning in fact will be considered first.

DISPOSITION OF APPEALS DECISIONS

Of the 70 appeals laid during the one-year period, 21 were decided in favor of the appellant.[55] This ratio of approximately one-third favorable results was consistent for all categories[56] and issues.[57] No significant variation in results could be attributed to the appellant's race.[58] Where the reason for the appeal was the sufficiency of budget (where the assistance was reduced or an increase denied), the results tended to show a somewhat lower rate of decision favorable to the appellant, with an average of 22 percent favorable, compared with 37 percent for other issues.[59] This is not surprising because the discretion of a caseworker in budget-determination cases is limited by quantified standards. In those cases, therefore, the opportunity for disagreement between caseworker and referee would be reduced relative to cases (such as those involved in special grants) where the caseworker has a high degree of discretion.

One variable that does seem to influence the results is the referee. Although the figures in Table 2.5 are small for most referees, it is clear that referee B was less willing than the others to overrule a caseworker's decision. Referee B found against the appellant in 21 of the 23 cases. The author was frequently surprised to read referee B's decisions, particularly as he showed apparent sympathy with, and courtesy toward, the appellants at the hearings. On the other hand, referee A, who appeared brusque at hearings, found in favor of the appellant in one-third of his decisions.

What do these case outcomes tell us about the possible success of an appeal? They indicate that about one in three appeals will be favorable to the appellant, with an even higher chance of a favorable appeal against a nonbudgetary determination, where the decision involves more discretion, and thus a greater opportunity for the referee to differ from the caseworker's determination. No other factor appeared to influence the chances of a successful outcome, except that one of the six referees seemed impervious to the arguments of appellants and consistently held against them.

Table 2.5 Disposition of Appeals by Referee

Referee	Favorable result		Unfavorable result		Total
	Percentage	N	Percentage	N	
A	31.2%	5	68.8%	11	16
B	9.5	2	90.5	19	21
C	62.5	5	37.5	3	8
D	15.4	2	84.6	11	13
E	75.0	3	25.0	1	4
F	50.0	2	50.0	2	4
Total	28.8%	19	71.2%	47	66

In the author's view, the appellants should have obtained a somewhat higher ratio of favorable decisions than the one of three that was in fact obtained. In five cases the referees failed to follow the law.[60] In four cases the referee simply failed to deal with some of the appellants' requests. In addition, the burden of proof was normally placed upon the appellant. For example, in cases where appellants claimed substitute checks for those that had been lost, the referee found that "the appellant has not proved that the check was not lost." Presumptions relating to the receipt of outside income were in all cases used against the appellant. For example, married children living with the appellant were presumed to have contributed to the "common household expenses" despite strong denials.[61]

In addition, the procedures on appeals were structured so as to allow an opportunity for the referee to be exposed to evidence that was irrelevant to the claim at issue and prejudicial to the appellant's case. Prior to an appeal the appellant's caseworker prepares a written summary of the issue to be determined. The referee would normally arrive at the district office shortly before the day's cases were due to be heard in order to read over each appellant's summary as well as her case file, which indicates all the dealings between the recipient and the caseworker including the caseworker's regular assessment of the recipient's personality, habits and household functioning. Furthermore, the caseworker would be able to justify her own decision through her summary or to insert remarks prejudicial to the appellant, such as the following:

"The client has a carpeted apartment and a T.V. set and a whirlpool washer" (in relation to the appellant's request for winter clothes for her children).

"The worker finds none of the client's complaints valid or realistic and feels the client is continuing a pattern of harassment of this department by the MAW organization."

'In the past this client used money given to her for back rental to send her son to summer camp."

"In the past this client has been given grants such as housekeeper services." (These services were in fact provided at a doctor's request. The summary failed to mention many instances of this client's past requests being refused.)

Even without remarks such as these in the case summary, the referee could be exposed to similar remarks written by the caseworker into the appellant's case record. For example:

"Client asks [for special grant]. She says her friends get more than she does. She is often irrational."

"This is the second time client claims to have lost her welfare check. She is welfare-wise."

A small number of social work supervisors were brazen in their attempts to influence the referee either before or after the hearing. After one hearing, for example, at which the appellant had made a good impression, the supervisor informed the referee that she frequently beat her child. In another case, the supervisor approached the referee prior to the hearing and said:

"The MAWS are after this woman and are pushing her. She doesn't give a straight story. I haven't seen this woman, but my social worker tells me that she will come in and make a good impression. She cries all the time."

On another occasion the same supervisor entered before the client was due in order to warn the referee that "she tells a different story every time."

Strict rules of evidence are not required for administrative hearings.[62] Nevertheless, the structure of the welfare appeals process would seem to be heavily weighted against the appellant. Despite the evidently "judicial" nature of the procedures, the referee does not view the appellant strictly as a "claimant" demanding "rights." Because of paternalistic concern, the referees think it legitimate to view the recipient as a "whole man,"[63] looking at his entire history, family functioning, and the full range of his problems. To take account of these factors in order to assess rehabilitative measures is understandable. To take them into account in order to determine liability or guilt in a "legal" setting will have the effect of exposing the referee to evidence strictly external to the question at issue and therefore strictly irrelevant to a determination of that question. The evidence was frequently prejudicial to the appellant, who was presented with no opportunity to view or rebut it.

THE APPEALS PROCEDURE AS EXPERIENCED BY APPELLANTS

The appellants interviewed, although otherwise representative of other recipients who had not appealed, showed greater knowledge of their legal rights.[64] Only one in four of the appellants gained a favorable decision (ten of forty interviewed).[65] However, three of every four appellants felt that their cases had been handled fairly. It would seem predictable that all but one of the successful appellants felt this way, but almost seven out of every ten unsuccessful appellants[66] also conceded the fairness of the appeals procedure.

When asked what they would do if they were unhappy with a caseworker's decision, just over one-half the appellants (23 of 42) volunteered that they would appeal again. Most of those who did not volunteer the appeal nevertheless considered that it would be worthwhile to challenge a caseworker at an appeal hearing (12 of the 19 felt this way).[67] Therefore only 1 in 6 (7 of the 42) were entirely negative about the use of the appeals procedure. Again, the appellant's view of the appeals procedure does not appear to be colored significantly by his own experience.[68]

Table 2.6 below shows the appellants' assessment of the usefulness of various possible avenues of protest against a caseworker's decision. The highest number of appellants (almost three out of every four) considered the appeal to be helpful, compared with one-half who considered persisting within the department or approaching the MAWS, and only one-third who would approach a lawyer.

Table 2.6 Welfare Appellants' Assessment of Usefulness of
Grievance Response:
*"Of the following things to do, which would be of use to a person who was unhappy with his or her social worker's decision, and wanted to get the decision changed?"**

	Appellants	
	Percentage	N
1. Appeal		
Helpful	71.4%	30
Not helpful	19.0	8
Don't know	9.6	4
Total	100.0	42
2. Persist Within the Department		
Helpful	54.8	23
Not helpful	33.3	14
Don't know	11.9	5
Total	100.0	42
3. Approach MAWS**		
Helpful	54.7	18
Not helpful	15.1	5
Don't know	30.2	10
Total	100.0	33
4. Approach a Lawyer		
Helpful	33.3	14
Not Helpful	45.3	19
Don't know	21.4	9
Total	100.0%	42

*Respondents were asked to provide the response "very helpful," "helpful," or "not very helpful." The tabulation "helpful" here includes "very helpful."
**Asked only of those who knew MAWS.

Although one in three of all appellants at the district office during the year obtained favorable decisions, only one in six of the appellants interviewed were themselves negative about the usefulness of the appeals procedure.[69] Over one-half would appeal again, and three-quarters considered the appeal a useful method of redress and their own appeal fair.

Although in the author's assessment more decisions might have been in favor of the appellants, the appellants themselves (who were not aware of the procedural irregularities or errors in law discussed above) appeared largely satisfied with the appeal as a method of redressing grievances.

The dissatisfaction of past participants in the appeals process is therefore probably not a factor contributing to any reluctance to initiate an appeal. In any event, the recipients interviewed were probably correct in their positive assessment of the usefulness of the appeals procedure to change caseworkers' decisions. At least one of every three decisions was altered through an appeal, and the appeal was frequently useful in bringing to light budgetary omissions or errors detrimental to the appellant.[70]

Again, we should distinguish the situation in practice from the prediction of what is likely to happen. In order to take the step of appealing, the recipient would have to believe that the hearing referee will be receptive to his argument and that the procedures will be fair.

Although most appellants interviewed believed that the procedures were fair, most welfare recipients will, according to the literature, be skeptical of the sympathy or goodwill of officials or will feel that they do not have the personal capacity or power to change things.[71] The responses elicited in the present study tend to confirm this attitude. Of the 13 recipients in Madison Park who claimed to be dissatisfied with their caseworker's decision, 9 took no further action to change that decision. We should interpret this statistic cautiously; the sample here was small, and the claim to be dissatisfied might have been imagined subsequently. However, we might note that the reasons given by 5 of the 9 for not taking action were grounded in skepticism or ignorance as reflected in the phrase, "There's nothing we can do," or "it's all politics." The other 4 were apathetic and "just never got around to it."

Even if a person does believe he may win his case, he will still weigh other costs before prosecuting an appeal. He will first consider the estimated time, effort and expenses involved in the appeal. The cost of remaining on welfare, and being subject to some of the controls over the recipient discussed above, may also be weighed. One factor in particular may cause the recipient to hesitate before challenging the caseworker's decision: At the hearing the caseworker and client will be adversaries. Except for an appeal from a determination concerning Disability Assistance, where the caseworker can impute responsibility for the decision to the State Medical Review Team,[72] the worker will appear at the hearing in the capacity of defendant, endeavoring to justify a decision which the client will contest. The hearing might well spark mutual antagonism. However, the client-caseworker relationship is likely to continue. Because the client is dependent upon her caseworker's goodwill for the basic necessities of life, it is natural that she will be wary of providing an opportunity for antagonism to develop between them.[75]

Observation of the appeal hearings supported the belief that both caseworker and client were aware of the hearing's potential threat to their ongoing relationship. One appellant complained to the hearing referee that she had been warned frequently by her caseworker that "to argue gets you nowhere." Partly to avoid client-caseworker antagonism, the Welfare Department was at times represented at a hearing by the caseworker's supervisor. However, the caseworker was usually present—to justify her decision. Numerous appeals provoked heated exchanges between caseworker and recipient—which could not have worked to the recipient's long-run advantage.

SUMMARY

We have seen in this chapter that many factors do, and others may, inhibit a welfare recipient's or applicant's appealing official decisions. Rights are not automatically triggered. In considering whether they will be effectively utilized, attitudes, resources, and relationships must be taken into account.

To start, knowledge of the law cannot be assumed; indeed, in most cases there is no opportunity to gain such knowledge. Furthermore, the individual's surrender to professional authority and dependence on the welfare relationship tend to stifle any questioning about legal rights. In addition, many people perceive welfare as a privilege, not a right. Even if the right were understood, the procedure for asserting it seems rarely to be known. And if the law and procedures are known, many welfare recipients are still unwilling to bear the costs (in terms of resources or relationships) of appealing— nor might they be optimistic about their chances of winning.

The welfare situation is, of course, a special one, and to a certain extent the implications of the findings must be confined to this situation. The implications concerning the control of bureaucracy, and ways in which obstacles to appeals may be overcome, will be considered in subsequent chapters.

Nevertheless, it may be suggested at this point that much of the evidence concerning the obstacles to the utilization of the appeals procedure remains valid in other situations, especially where the potential beneficiaries of rights possess social, economic, or cultural characteristics in common with welfare recipients. Chapter 3 considers further evidence on this question.

Law and Bureaucracy

Notes

1. The interviewers were of the same race as the appellants. Fifty percent of the sample was (by random selection) black. The respondents were not aware of the author's involvement in the survey. The 42 appellants were randomly selected.

2. For a history of public assistance in Massachusetts and the Poor Laws generally, see R. Kelso, *The History of Public Poor Relief in Massachusetts, 1620-1920* (1922).

3. *Ibid.*, at 93.

4. *Ibid.*, at 117.

5. The Board of State Charities, a supervisory body was set up in 1863, *Mass. Senate Doc.* No. 2 (1863). In 1913 the Massachusetts Legislature passed an act allowing the overseers of the poor to assist mothers support their dependent children in their own homes. *Mass. Acts of 1913*, c.763. For the history of Massachusetts aid to dependent children, see Town of Cohasset v. Town of Scituate, 309 Mass. 402, 34 N.E. 2d 699 (1941). Assistance to the aged was first established in 1930. *Mass Acts of 1930*, § 402. For the history of Massachusetts aid to the aged, see City of Boston v. Commonwealth, 322 Mass. 181, 76 N.E. 2d 123 (1948).

6. 42 U.S.C. § § 301-1394 (1964) as amended (Supp. I, 1965). For an account of the legislative history see P. Douglas, *Social Security in the United States* (1935).

7. *Mass. Acts of 1935*, c. 494. From 1935 to 1960 the state received $754 million in federal disbursements under the act. See D. Cronin, "The Impact of Federal Welfare Grants on Municipal Government," 40 *B. U. L. Rev.* 531, 540 (1960).

8. See generally, J. Wedemeyer and P. Moore, "The American Welfare System," 54 *Calif. L. Rev.* 326 (1966). The federal act allows the states to determine their own standards. The principal conditions for receiving the grants-in-aid are: (1) statewide operation; (2) state financial participation; (3) administration by a single state agency; (4) maintenance of personal standards on a merit basis; (5) protection of the confidentiality of records; (6) opportunity for a fair hearing within a reasonable time; (7) submission of reports as required by the Department of Health, Education, and Welfare; (8) limits of imposition of residency restrictions. See Wedemeyer and Moore, *op. cit.*, p. 347.

9. See U.S. Department of Health, Education and Welfare *Handbook of Public Assistance Administration* (1966). Hereinafter *HEW Manual*.

10. Wedmeyer and Moore, *op. cit.*, 338-41 (1966).

11. The manual is only available in the offices of the state and local welfare departments. In Massachusetts General Hospital v. Commissioner of Public Welfare, 346 Mass. 739, 196 N.E. 2d 181 (1964), it was held that the state department of Public Welfare must hold public hearings before adopting the regulations.

12. *Mass. Gen. Laws* c. 118A (Supp. 1966) and *Massachusetts Public Assistance Policy Manual*, c. 1, §A (hereinafter, *Mass. Manual*).

13. *Mass. Manual*, c. 1, §§ A-E.

14. *Ibid.*, c. 1, §C, p. 3; and *Mass. Gen. Laws*, c. 118D (Supp. 1966).

15. Recent amendments to the federal act have allowed either parent to qualify. 76 Stat. 185 (1962), *as amended*; 42 U.S.C., §§601-609 (1964), *as amended*; 42 U.S.C., §§602, 603, 606 (Supp. I, 1965).

16. *Mass. Gen. Laws*, c. 118 (Supp. 1966); *Mass. Manual*, c. 1, §D.

17. *Mass. Gen. Laws*, c. 117, §1 (Supp. 1966).

18. In spite of the new "simplified budget" effective since October 1966. (Incorporated in the *Mass. Manual, op. cit.*)

19. To cover food, rent, fuel and utilities, household supplies, clothing, personal care, and life insurance.

20. If she lived in public housing, she would be allowed her rental plus $123.80 per month. For nonpublic housing there is a maximum rent the department will pay, e.g., $49 per month for a four-room heated apartment.

21. *Mass. Manual*, c IV, §A, p. 3.

22. National Study Service, *Meeting the Problems of People in Massachusetts*, at 11 (1965). In November 1965, 218,000 individuals in the state received assistance in Massachusetts. Just under half of these received AFDC.

23. Welfare Department, City of Boston, *Monthly Financial and Statistical Reports*.

24. *Ibid.* The breakdown of categories in the district office was as follows: OAA, 2437; MA, 2680; AFDC, 2880; DA, 765; GR, 684.

25. *Ibid.*

26. Eligibility for DA will normally be assessed by the State Medical Review Team (SMRT), whose membership includes qualified medical personnel. *Mass. Manual*, c. I, §C, p. 7. A person too ill or disabled to go to the office may request an interview at home.

27. *Mass. Gen. Laws*, c. 118, §4 (Supp. 1966).

28. *Mass. Manual*, c. VI. This section also provides that the appellant shall be informed of his right to counsel in accordance with recent federal regulations, contained in the *HEW Manual* Transmittal No. 56, s. IV-6200 (3)(e).

29. By 62 appellants. Some appellants appealed twice, and others appealed on more than one issue.

30. All figures in this section will be tabulated from cases observed in the present study supplemented by the monthly *Statistical Reports* of the City of Boston, Welfare Department, Research and Statistics Section.

31. The breakdown of appeals was as follows: Applications denied, 18.6% (13); assistance withdrawn, 11.4% (8); assistance reduced, 25.7% (18); increase denied, 20% (14); special grant denied, 24.3% (17). Cf. J.

Handler, "Justice for the Welfare Recipient: Fair Hearings in AFDC—The Wisconsin Experience," 43 *Social Service Rev.* 12 (1969).

32. The denials for categories were OAA, 14%; MA, 18.3%; AFDC, 6.5%; DA, 27.7%, and GR, 5.2%.

33. Such figures are not available for the district office, but no evidence suggests that they would show any significantly different patterns.

34. Approximately 1% of the total, but 8% of all OAA applications.

35. Thirty-nine % of all denied applications were accounted for on this basis.

36. This figure supports the Wisconsin experience and Handler's interpretation of it (*op. cit.*, at 24), that OAA and DA applicants have more of the resources necessary to challenge government authority than AFDC applicants because they are recent members of the labor force, with experience in handling their own affairs.

37. Handler, *op. cit.*, at 20, found that 1.2% of all denials of AFDC in Wisconsin resulted in appeals.

38. One reason for this is the three-month limit for general relief.

39. In Boston during the period of this study 60% of withdrawals were from OAA and MA cases (for the obvious reason of age and health) but only 3.5% of AFDC cases.

40. About 40% of AFDC cases in Boston were withdrawn due to the failure of the recipient to continue contact. The figure for other categories was approximately 15% in all cases.

41. Handler, *op. cit.*, at 20, found that 0.4% of AFDC cases withdrawn in Wisconsin were appealed.

42. Seventy of 9500 total caseload at the district office. The figure in Handler's sample was 1 in 1000 over a 20-year period. Handler, *op. cit.*, at 20.

43. Only 3% of 15% of Handler's sample who were dissatisfied with a decision appealed. *Ibid.*, at 26-27 (1969).

44. *Ibid.*

45. In Banner v. Smolenski et al. U.S. District Court, Civ. Action No. 69, 1053-8 (October 7, 1969) (unreported), CCH *Pov. L. Rev.*, ss. 10, 587 (1969), the Massachusetts District Court issued a temporary restraining order to delay a hearing until the recipient and her attorney were furnished with a copy of the case summary and complete record.

46. For an account of the movement of the philosophy of welfare away from the virtues of support (largely in kind) for the "deserving poor," see J. Handler and A. Goldstein, "The Legislative Development of Public Assistance," 1 *Wisc. L. Rev.* 414 (1968).

47. See U.S. Department of Health, Education, and Welfare, *Report on the Task Force on the Organization of the Social Services, Services for People* (October 15, 1968). In 1956 and 1962 the Social Security Act was amended to provide (in addition to income-maintenance programs) "rehabilitation and other services" for AFDC families "to help maintain and strengthen family life" and to help families "attain or retain capability for the maximum self-support and personal

independence." 42 U.S.C. 601, as amended, 1962. See G. Steiner, *Social Insecurity: The Politics of Welfare*, chap. 2 (1966).

48. The term "basic budgeted need" specifically excludes "leisure time activities." *Mass. Manual*, chap. IV, p. 2.

49. E. Hollis and A. Taylor, *Social Work Education in the United States*, at 205-206 (1951). See also A. Keith Lucas, *Decisions About People in Need*, at 69 (1957).

50. See. E. Sparer, "Social Welfare Law Testing," 12 *Prac. Law* 14 (1966); C. Reich, "Midnight Welfare Searches and the Social Security Act," 72 *Yale L.J.* 1347 (1963).

51. The practice was held unconstitutional by the U.S. Supreme Court in Smith v. King, 88 *Sup. Cr.* 2128 (1968).

52. *Ibid.*, chap. 2, Section A, p. 6. In addition, the use of police badges or other equipment or of police personnel is prohibited.

53. See S. Briar, "Welfare From Below: Recipients' View of the Public Welfare System," 54 *Calif. L. Rev.* 370, 380 (1966); R. O'Neill, "Unconstitutional Conditions: Welfare Benefits with Strings Attached," 54 *Calif. L. Rev.* 370 (1966).

54. This figure is lower than that revealed in surveys by Briar and Handler, where one-third of the recipients did not know where to appeal. Briar, *op. cit.*, at 379-380; J. Handler, "Justice for the Welfare Recipient: Fair Hearings in AFDC—The Wisconsin Experience," 43 *Social Service Rev.* 12, 28 (March 1969).

55. Cf. Handler, *op. cit.*, at 22, who found that 45% of appeals in Wisconsin resulted in a determination favorable to the appellant.

56. Of all cases appealed, 51.6% were in the AFDC category. The others were 29.0% DA, 12.9% OAA, and 6.5% MA.

57. Forty percent of all issues (28) involved an increase in budget or special grant; 38.5% (27) involved the question of an appellant's resources (e.g., should her savings or daughter's earnings be taken into account); 11.5% (8) constituted procedural issues (such as the appellant's failure to present a doctor's certificate) and 10% (7) involved medical questions in DA or MAA cases.

58. Twenty-nine of the appellants were black, 33 white.

59. Seven of 32 sufficiency of budget cases were determined favorably to the appellant, as compared with 14 of 38 other cases.

60. For example, in Massachusetts General Hospital v. Commissioner of Public Welfare, 216 N.E. 2d 434 (1966), it was held that the referee's decision based on the advice of the State Medical Review Board (SMRT) "does not constitute substantial evidence," since the SMRT's evidence was not presented to the referee at the hearing. This decision appeared to be generally ignored. In one case the referee ignored the case of Fenton v. Dept. of Welfare, 344 Mass. 343, 182 N.E. 2d 528, where it was held that the Board of Welfare was without authority to deny the applicant DA solely because her father, who, if he possessed sufficient resources would be responsible for her support, failed to furnish the Department with information of his financial situation.

61. Irrefutable presumptions such as these might be considered unconstitutional. As has been said in a tax case, e.g.,: "We have no doubt that, because of the fundamental conceptions which underlie our system, any attempt by a state to measure the tax on one person's property or income by reference to the property or income of another is contrary to the due process of law as guaranteed by the fourteenth amendment. That which is not in fact the taxpayer's income cannot be made such by calling it income. . . ." Hoeper v. Tax Commissioner, 284 U.S. 206, 215 (1931). Accord, Heiner v. Donnan, 285 U.S. 312 (1932).

62. "We . . . recognize the importance of not imposing upon the States or the Federal Government in this developing field of law any procedural requirements beyond those demanded by rudimentary due process." Mr. Justice Brennan, in Goldberg v. Kelly, 90 S. Ct. 1011 (1970).

63. Nonet's account of Workman's Compensation in California shows a similar pattern during the "first stage" of the Commission's history. P. Nonet, *Administrative Justice* (1969).

64. Sixty-five percent of the appellants but only one-half of other recipients thought that the law gave a right to welfare if income was sufficiently low; 26% of the appellants (compared with 40% of nonappellant recipients) thought (wrongly) that a caseworker had a right to enter a recipient's home at any time; 28% of the appellants (compared with 60% of the other recipients) thought (wrongly) that the law gave a caseworker the right to know how welfare recipients spent their money.

65. Two appellants of the 42 withdrew their appeal prior to decision.

66. Eighteen of 26.

67. Sixteen of these 19 (38.1% of the total sample) would have persisted within the welfare department; 1 would consult a lawyer, 1 would consult the MAWS, and 1 would do nothing.

68. Of the 7 appellants negative to the appeals system, 3 had obtained a favorable decision. Of the 35 favorable to the appeal, 26 had obtained an unfavorable decision.

69. One in four of the sample interviewed obtained favorable decisions.

70. For example, in two cases, the referee, in considering the facts of a case, discovered that one child of the appellant had been fortuitously omitted from her budget, and was not being provided for. In six other cases it was discovered that the worker was ignorant of the correct rule—e.g., that a husband's support could be paid direct to the department, that DA recipients could also receive AFDC, that an applicant for assistance could become eligible by assigning an insurance policy to the Department.

71. Briar (*op. cit.*, at 379-380) found that even though a welfare recipient in California was informed of his right to appeal, this

information was not meaningful to a person who conceived of himself as a suppliant. Under these circumstances the information may be ignored or soon forgotten.

72. This point does not apply to appeals lodged, e.g., by a hospital against the payment of certain medical expenses. See Springfield Hospital v. Commissioner of Public Welfare, 216 N.E. 2d 440 (1966).

73. This point is made in J. Handler, "Controlling Official Behavior in Welfare Administration," 54 *Calif. L. Rev.* 479 (1966). This factor would, of course, prove less of a deterrent to applicants than to recipients.

3

Complaints to Bureaucracy: Antidiscrimination Laws

Continuing our examination of obstacles to access to bureaucracy, this chapter considers the situation where an individual seeks redress for a private wrong. In this case the complainant is challenging racial discrimination allegedly perpetrated by a private individual, firm or corporation rather than an official organization.

ORGANIZATIONAL STRUCTURE AND PROCEDURES

In 1946 Massachusetts established the Fair Employment Practices Commission to enforce a law prohibiting racial discrimination in employment.[1] Subsequently, the commission's jurisdiction was expanded,[2] and its name was changed to the Massachusetts Commission against Discrimination (MCAD).[3] The MCAD consists of four commissioners[4] and a staff and at the time of this study had offices in downtown Boston and Springfield. The analysis here will consider complaints laid in 1965 at the Boston office, which alleged racial discrimination in housing and employment.

A complaint may be filed by any person claiming to be aggrieved by an unlawful discriminatory practice or by his attorney, the state attorney general, or the MCAD.[5] Except for the issues of discriminatory advertisements or application forms, the MCAD proved reluctant to issue its own complaints.[6] Only 10 were initiated by the MCAD in 1965.[7] Individuals filed 126 complaints alleging racial discrimination in housing[8] and 94 in employment.[9]

A complainant must appear at the MCAD's offices,[10] where he is interviewed by a field representative who notarizes the complaint[11] and gathers "supplementary information"[12] intended to reveal the suitability of the complainant for the housing or employment in question. Each case is assigned to one commissioner.

Within a few days the field representative begins investigation of the allegation,[13] normally presenting himself to the respondent without prior warning, merely stating upon arrival that he represents the state, and stressing his impartiality. Information about the racial composition of the area or firm in question is assembled. The field representative then checks the respondent's explanation for his conduct.[14] For example, should the respondent say that the complainant was rejected because he failed to produce suitable credit references, the field representative ascertains whether the complainant had, in fact, failed to produce the references and whether the same qualification was demanded of other applicants or occupants of the housing or employment in question.

Once the investigatory report is completed, the assigned commissioner determines whether there is probable cause of discrimination,[15] sometimes calling an "investigatory conference" in order better to assess the facts.[16] It will be seen below that the findings of the commissioners vary widely, corresponding to their individual conceptions of the purpose of the law and their own functions.[17]

Should the commissioner find lack of probable cause, the case is closed and the complainant has no right of appeal. Should a finding of probable cause be found, however, the commissioner "shall immediately endeavor to eliminate the unlawful practice complained of ... by conference, conciliation, and persuasion."[18] A conciliation agreement might ideally serve four purposes: first, relief to the complainant (in the form of an offer of the employment or housing in question or compensatory damages); second, elimination of any other discriminatory practice discovered; third, deterrence of other discrimination in the community (i.e., by means of publicity); and fourth, prevention of future discrimination on the part of the respondent (by means of an undertaking or other commitment).

However, a conciliation agreement might not be honored by a respondent, and the MCAD has neither the time nor the resources to test whether it is adhered to. The commission was reluctant to insist that the respondents produce periodic "compliance reports," and as a result the respondent was not obliged to prove his compliance.[20]

It is doubtful whether most conciliation agreements could be enforced by the MCAD. In one case, involving a respondent's second offence, the respondent signed a consent decree, but this procedure is unlikely to become regular.[21] Should a respondent fail to accept the terms of conciliation, however, the commission can proceed to a public hearing. Because only eight hearings were held in 1965, their effect as a sword is largely Damoclean.[22] Unlike conciliation agreements, the orders issued after a public hearing may be enforced through contempt proceedings in the courts.[23]

OBSTACLES TO THE INITIATION OF COMPLAINTS

Although the commission has the power to lay its own complaints, this is rarely done. Thus the commission, like a court, will in most cases wait passively until a complaint is laid before initiating enforcement proceedings. It has been said that enforcement of the law through the initiation of individual complaints is like trying to "drain a swamp with a teaspoon,"[24] and critics have complained that the MCAD does not lay its own complaints in strategic areas.

This study will not deal directly with the problem of strategic enforcement of the antidiscrimination laws, although obstacles to individual complaints might affect this too. Instead it will focus on the factors that might inhibit or deter individuals from complaining to the MCAD about discrimination.

What was the rate of complaints to the MCAD in proportion to the total rate of discrimination in Boston? Clearly this figure is impossible to discover. Thus we can be far less sure than with welfare appeals that the process is underutilized. However, one piece of evidence is revealed in the present study: Of 20 blacks who claimed to have been discriminated against in the past, only one had complained about the alleged discrimination to the MCAD. One other had complained to a labor union, and the rest had taken no action at all.

Some understanding of those who do *not* complain might be gleaned from an analysis of the characteristics of those who do. We might try to discover whether the average complainant is representative of the average person discriminated against in Boston.

In his study of the MCAD's operations in 1959/60, Leon Mayhew found that in employment cases "the structure of complaints" did not correspond with the "structure of discrimination."[25] Mayhew is referring to the fact that employment complaints were not representative of the main manifestations of discrimination at that time. He found that most employment complaints were laid against racially integrated firms, where the degree of discrimination was not as great as that in predominantly or completely white firms. In housing, by contrast, Mayhew found that the structure of complaints and discrimination did coincide, because most complaints were laid with respect to housing in the predominantly or completely white suburbs, which, Mayhew assumes, were also the areas of greatest discrimination.

We should not, however, assume that areas of racial imbalance and areas of racial discrimination are necessarily coincidental.[26] Reports on Boston, for example, have suggested that, in fact, the areas of greatest discrimination may not be areas of greatest racial imbalance. It has been said that areas on the outer edge of the black sections of Boston, which are predominantly but not exclusively white, "where whites feel the thrust of a spreading ghetto, are the most difficult in which to establish an interest in or understanding of fair housing."[27] The most highly segregated areas of housing in Boston, therefore, are probably not those with as much discrimination, in fact or potentially, as in Boston's less segregated, but racially changing, areas. It therefore seems that housing complaints—because they were laid against areas of greatest racial imbalance—were not representative of the "structure" of discrimination.

Table 3.1 shows that over one-half of the complainants were attempting to move out of all-black or changing areas. Although only 16 percent alleged discrimination in changing areas, where the highest incidence of discrimination occurs, Table 3.2 shows that the majority were applying for housing in white areas—where discrimination is probably less.[28]

The average housing complaint is therefore unlikely to be representative of the typical discriminatory situation. The personal characteristics of housing complainants bear out this hypothesis. Their mean family income in 1965 was $6768 per year, more than 50 percent higher than that of the average Boston black family in 1960 of $4383.[29] The average rental of housing for which blacks applied was $101 per month, almost 50 percent higher than the average rent paid by blacks in 1960 of $78 per month.[30] The average purchase price of a home was $17,200.

In summary, we know that only one in twenty blacks interviewed who had alleged discrimination actually lodged a complaint with the MCAD. This evidence should be cautiously interpreted. However, the characteristics of the average complainant to the MCAD tend to confirm the hypothesis: The average complainant was not representative of the average black in Boston. We cannot be certain that he was unrepresentative of the average black discriminated against, but it would seem that most discrimination took place in areas poorer than those for which the average housing complainant was applying.

Table 3.1   Location of Housing Complainants by Area

1. Nature of the area in which the complainant was living at the time of the complaint

Area	Percentage complaints (N = 85)
All black	44.66%
Changing*	10.71
Integrated	16.05
Predominantly white	14.29
All white	14.29
Total	100.00%

2. Nature of the area of the property that was the subject of the dispute before the MCAD

Area	Percentage complaints (N = 85)
All black	1.80%
Changing*	16.07
Integrated	7.14
Predominantly white	17.85
All white	57.14
Total	100.00%

*Changing from all black to integrated.

Complaints to Bureaucracy: Antidiscrimination Laws

Various steps must be taken before a person can file a complaint about discrimination. First, the person must expose himself to discrimination; second, he must recognize (or imagine) that discrimination has taken place; third, he must know what action to take; and fourth, he must be willing (and able) to take action. These four steps will be considered in the light of information drawn from the literature and interviews with residents of the Madison Park area of Boston (63 of whom were black) and 21 black welfare appellants. This sample is not perfectly representative of blacks in Boston.[31] However, the attitudes of the welfare appellants showed no significant variation from those shown by the Madison Park sample, and where independent variables such as income or education affect the result, this will be shown. We should, nevertheless, be cautious about claiming that the attitudes are anything more than suggestive. In addition, the results of interviews with MCAD complainants will be presented. That sample consisted of 35 MCAD housing complainants selected randomly from 85 complaints closed in 1965.

Exposure to Discrimination

An individual may be exposed to discrimination in various ways: at times merely from being an employee who is discharged or fails to receive promotion or upgrading, or from being a tenant who is evicted or subjected to discriminatory conditions. In these cases the respondent will have already hired at least one black employee or accepted one black tenant. In most cases, however, the individual will first have to apply for employment or housing, and many factors might militate against blacks applying where they are likely to encounter discrimination.

It might be said that if a person is not personally aggrieved by a discriminatory act, then no problem exists in terms of access or underutilization of a law. However, it is important to recognize that forces may prevent a person's even being in a position to challenge an illegal situation. An analogy in the welfare situation may be drawn with the case of a welfare recipient who fails even to request an allowable item, with the mistaken view that such items are not allowable, at least to her. Failure by a claimant to assert a right would allow the welfare department to avoid a direct refusal of that right.

If, however, potential beneficiaries of rights have no desire to avail themselves of their rights, then no problem arises. For example, welfare recipients could have no desire to avail themselves of the right to an annual winter coat, and blacks may have no desire to avail themselves of the right to live or work in a white area.

Research into the middle-income black family in Boston revealed that "many Negroes, like the members of other minorities in the United States, enjoy living close to and with others of their own origin, and appreciate a measure of continued Negro life."[32] Less than 5 percent of 234 black families interviewed by that survey felt that they would be most comfortable living in a white community. Other research has hypothesized that some blacks might have developed a vested interest in segregation and for commercial, ideological, or political reasons might not wish to leave Boston's predominantly black Roxbury area.[33]

This conclusion, however, was not confirmed by the attitude survey undertaken for this study. As Table 3.2 shows, over one-half of those interviewed stated their explicit preference for an integrated neighborhood. Another quarter stated they had no preference. Only 14.4 percent of blacks (as opposed to 35 percent of whites) stated their preference for a segregated area for members of their own race.[34] Thus we cannot unquestioningly accept the hypothesis that most blacks were eager to remain in predominantly segregated neighborhoods.

Apart from preference, many forces combine to prevent the initiation of antidiscrimination laws against violators by inhibiting or avoiding the challenge of a discriminatory situation. The average person would probably not wish to be humiliated or rebuffed when seeking housing and might fear the treatment of white neighbors toward himself and his children. Interviews with MCAD complainants revealed, however, that those living in integrated areas had in fact been

Table 3.2   Preferred Living Area: Blacks and Whites

Preferred area	Black Percentage	N	White Percentage	N
All black	14.4%	16	0.0%	0
Half and half	56.8	63	29.8	11
No preference	26.1	29	35.1	13
All white	2.7	3	35.1	13
Total	100.0%	111	100.0%	37

well received by their white neighbors and that they would prefer to continue living in a racially integrated area. This fact, however, might bear little relation to a potential applicant's expectation of living in a white area. In some cases before the MCAD, for example, the complainant was offered an apartment in an all-white area but was afraid to move in. In one case this fear was prompted by insults received from neighbors when he originally applied. In another case the complainant became afraid, without specific evidence, that her children might be harmed by the prejudice and discrimination in the area.

In employment, too, the major bastions of discrimination are often unchallenged because of the unwillingness of potential applicants to encounter expected discrimination or prejudice on the job. Few people have the motivation, energy, or resilience to be pioneers, at least in a work or housing situation.

In addition, due to the effects of past discrimination, segregation, and inferior schooling, blacks as a group are less "objectively" qualified than whites for many higher-level positions.[35] Mayhew's study makes the point that "structural" or "passive" discrimination allows a "color-blind management [to] let the established social structure do the work of discrimination, leaving clear consciences."[36] Apart from education, some of these structural forces are based on recruitment patterns in industry (firms perpetuating the racial composition of their work force by relying on new openings to be filled by word-of-mouth referrals) and the interaction between the housing market and the level of black employment.[37] For example, in Boston the inability of many blacks to find housing in their price range near the newly developing industrial location (along Route 128) inhibits black employment there.[38]

Recognition of Discrimination

The second move necessary to trigger the law-enforcement mechanism is for an individual to recognize (or imagine that he recognizes) discrimination. The blacks interviewed were asked if they had encountered discrimination in the past five years. About one in every four (20 of 84) said that they had. However, these figures should be cautiously interpreted. Perception of discrimination may or may not have any relation to real discrimination because various psychological factors may arise, causing a person to attribute an incident—for example, a rejection from employment—to discrimination. Similarly, psychological factors may prevent a person from recognizing discrimination against himself. Kenneth Clark has observed that

middle-class Negroes who break out of the ghetto are often themselves convinced that they are already accepted by whites—to be a test case would allow race to become salient in one's life, to bring the ghetto nightmare along when all one has sought is effective escape.[39]

We might simply note that discrimination may be subtle and difficult to detect and that an individual may for many reasons suppress or repress its existence.[40] For example, blacks have at times come to the commission to complain of discrimination on the ground of age when an obvious case of racial discrimination had taken place.[41]

Knowledge of the Commission

Suppose that a person exposed to discrimination perceives it as having occurred. Would he know what to do about it?

When asked whether they knew of the MCAD, only one-third of those interviewed claimed such knowledge, with the young and poorly educated displaying even greater ignorance.[42] When asked what action could be taken to challenge discrimination, the responses, tabulated in Table 3.3, show that 30 percent thought no action was possible, and only 16 percent mentioned the MCAD as a possible avenue of challenge. Those who complained to a civil rights organization, a politician, or a lawyer might be referred to the MCAD. However, the fact that only one in seven of those interviewed knew of the MCAD's function suggests a serious lack of knowledge among those whom the MCAD is supposed to serve.

Table 3.3 Action in Response to:
"If a person ran into discrimination tomorrow, in connection with a job or housing, what would he be able to do about it?"

Response	Percentage	N
No action possible	29.6%	24
Take action		
Organization (e.g., NAACP)	18.6	14
MCAD	16.0	13
Politicians (e.g., mayor, senator)	14.8	12
Legal Action (e.g., see a lawyer)	11.1	9
Complain (nonspecific)	9.9	8
	70.4	57
Total	100.0%	81

The Willingness to Complain

As noted, the decision to initiate legal action involves a rational calculation of the complainant's chances of success and a feeling that any potential benefits are worth the costs of time and effort. Before considering the reasons why people might not complain, or might not consider complaint worthwhile, we must discover the actual rate of success for those who did complain and the complainants' views of the procedure.

OUTCOME OF CASES BEFORE THE MCAD, 1965

In 1965 the Boston office of the MCAD processed 85 housing cases[43] and 45 employment cases.[44] Table 3.4 shows the results of the cases closed during the year.

Complaints to Bureaucracy: Antidiscrimination Laws

Table 3.4 shows that almost one in five of the complainants received the housing or employment that was the subject of their complaint, and another 36 percent were offered positions but declined to take them. Although it would seem that more than one-half of the complainants were in fact

Table 3.4   Final Disposition of Cases Closed Before the MCAD in 1965

	Percentage	N
Complainant receives housing or employment complained of[a]	18.8%	23
Complainant declined offer of housing or employment	36.1	44
Respondent agrees to offer complainant next available opening	1.6	2
Respondent writes letters indicating intention to comply with the law[b]	25.4	31
Respondent takes affirmative action	13.1	16
No action taken	5.0	6
Total	100.0%	122

[a]Includes 1 condition of employment changed.
[b]Includes 1 consent decree.

successful, responses to the questionnaire by complainants who refused offers to accept housing indicate that the reason for the refusals lay most often in the fact that the offer was wholly unsatisfactory to the needs of the complainant. For example:

"He offered to build a house like the one I wanted but on a back street that was undeveloped and where I didn't want to live."

"He offered me a house that was just inconvenient."

"He offered me a small, decrepit, unsuitable place."

At times too the brush with discrimination would make the

complainant apprehensive about moving into the area,[45] fearing future discrimination from neighbors.

In one of every four cases, the respondent wrote a "compliance letter"—in most cases to the complainant, sometimes to the commission, indicating his intention to obey the law in the future. Sometimes respondents took other action as well.

In 13.1 percent of the cases, the respondent agreed to take some degree of affirmative action. In housing cases this included an agreement to refer future vacancies to the MCAD, to display the MCAD poster, or to meet with civil rights organizations to discuss ways of broadening advertising sources. In employment cases the affirmative action included agreements to offer the next available opening to a black, to broaden sources of recruitment, or to alter procedures so as to stipulate the race of job applicants in order to increase black employment.

How successful were these cases from the point of view of the complainants?[46] One of every three cases was successful in that either the complainant got what he wanted or the respondent agreed to take affirmative action. Another 36 percent were successful in that the complainant was offered housing or employment by the respondent; but here the offer was frequently made in bad faith.

THE MCAD PROCEDURES AS
EXPERIENCED BY THE COMPLAINANTS

More than three of every four complainants interviewed made consistently favorable statements about their experience before the MCAD. Twenty-six of the 35 interviewed thought that the MCAD was doing a good job and was useful in improving conditions for blacks in Massachusetts. The same number were satisfied with the outcome of their cases before the MCAD. Twenty-eight of the 35 thought their cases had been handled fairly. As would be expected, all those who obtained the desired housing were favorably disposed toward the MCAD and the procedures in their cases. However, even those whose cases were unsuccessful were evenly divided.[47]

The reasons for the positive responses varied. Some considered that the MCAD had simply been personally helpful. Others were impressed with the operations and strategies of the MCAD in general, as shown in the following remarks:

"They take legal action that I could not afford."

"They put strong pressure on a defendant that I could not do alone."

Those with negative views of the MCAD expressed disappointment with its defective strategies or its inefficient or tardy action—particularly during the investigation of a complaint—as illustrated below:

"They don't tackle skilled jobs, where the money is" (examples given from electrical unions).

"They revealed their position [to the respondent] and allowed him time to prepare excuses and find loopholes."

"They let [the respondent realtor] off the hook too lightly."

"They should handle similar cases together and work with a group that wants to get into an area to buy houses there."

A large majority of the complainants were, therefore, favorably disposed toward the MCAD. When asked what the worst things about the MCAD were, 15 of the 35 refused to answer the question on the ground that there were no bad things about it. Thirty-one of the 35 said that if discriminated against in the future they would again complain to the MCAD.

These responses indicate that it would be wrong to attribute blame for the deficiencies in antidiscrimination laws to the method of administration by the officials—at least as their operations are seen through the eyes of the complainants. Even if the complainants interviewed could be said to have been overenthusiastic about the MCAD's qualities, at least one in three obtained successful results from his complaint. The way the antidiscrimination law is administered should not, therefore, act as a deterrent to its use.

However, as observed in connection with the initiation of welfare appeals, the claimant's *assessment* of the situation, not the situation in fact, determines the likelihood of his initiating action. What reasons might inhibit the laying of a complaint of discrimination, once the discrimination is recognized and the feasibility of complaint is understood?

A common attitude in the face of discrimination is resignation;[48] a feeling that to protest is futile or simply not worth the time and effort. Fear of retaliation may also inhibit the laying of complaints.[49]

Another reason for failure to protest could be the existence of attitudes similar to those Gans observed in the Italian community in Boston's West End. A number of black writers such as Malcom X, Claude Brown, and James Baldwin have reported that in New York's Harlem law is viewed as a tool used by the white world against blacks. A survey of the attitude of blacks in New Jersey toward law concluded that *all* institutions designed to aid blacks were rejected by them as inadequate, including black action groups, social workers, the educational system, and political power—as well as the judicial system.[50]

This study attempted to verify these hypotheses. Of the individuals who claimed to know of the MCAD, only about one in seven[51] said they would not complain to the commission if discriminated against. Survey results indicate, however, that a person's actions might not correspond to his intentions when he is faced with discrimination. Of the twenty who claimed to have been discriminated against in the five years prior to the interview (March 1968), only two actually took action: One of them complained to his labor union, the other to the MCAD.

Why did the remaining 18 not take action about the discrimination? Many reasons, including lack of a substantial complaint, could account for the failure. However, the replies are indicative of potential reasons for which the laying of complaints might be inhibited. Four respondents stated that they had insufficient evidence of discrimination, five thought that action would not help because "you can't change peoples' prejudices," two thought they needed money to initiate action, and the remaining seven did not know where to go (three of these thought that they could complain to their state representative but did not know how to set this in motion).[52]

All blacks interviewed were asked which of the following courses of action was the best way for blacks in Boston to try to do away with discrimination. The choices were: getting better education, trying to get new laws passed, peaceful public demonstrations (like picketing or marching), trying to get the existing laws properly enforced, praying to change men's hearts, and violence. The results are tabulated in Table 3.5 below.

Table 3.5   Action in Response to Discrimination

Action	Percentage	N
Education	60.6%	72
Law	22.6	27
Enforcing present laws	14.2	17
New laws	8.4	10
Other	16.8	20
Prayer	10.1	12
Peaceful protest	4.2	5
Violence	2.5	3
Total	100.0%	119

Table 3.5 shows that over 60 percent of blacks interviewed considered improving their educational position the preferred

means to reduce discrimination. Over 1 in 5 favored legal means, and only 3 of the sample of 119 favored violence. Not surprisingly, education was favored more by those with low educational status themselves and by those of lower occupational levels.[53] More people with higher educational status presumably considered that their education would not serve to protect them from discrimination. Prayer was favored more by older people.

What do these responses tell us? Insofar as we can—cautiously—generalize from this sample, it seems that the enforcement of antidiscrimination laws is not seen by blacks as a primary means of fighting discrimination. Education is considered the most effective means, and violence the least effective. The enforcement of existing laws is considered of primary importance for only about one in seven (14.2 percent).

The responses to these questions were received with disbelief by colleagues. After all, in April 1968, following the assassination of Dr. Martin Luther King, just one month after this survey was taken, riots broke out in the predominantly black area of Boston. Only adults were interviewed, however. Advocates of violence may not have been a part of the sample—or even available for an interview. Further, violence might be sparked spontaneously and perhaps is *not* premeditated (or admitted) as a preferred course of action. These tabulations are presented, therefore, as an indication of the views expressed by those interviewed at one point in time. No prediction of future protest patterns can be gleaned from them. The responses, however, are consistent with the findings above: They show little enthusiasm for law as a strategy to combat discrimination and a good deal of skepticism that bureaucracy will enforce the law fairly and vigorously.

SUMMARY

Analysis of MCAD processes reveals much about obstacles to

access to law and bureaucracy. In the welfare situation, attitudes, resources, and relationships must be considered in assessing whether laws will be utilized. Complaints were laid to bureaucracy about previous decisions, but the continuing relationship between the complainant and the decision maker proved to inhibit the potential complainant from pursuing her rights. Although this variable was not present in the MCAD situation, we discover many similar constraints. A law may tend to induce obedience by the fact of its existence. Many blacks, however, may not wish to utilize antidiscrimination laws, preferring to live and work among their own race. The first of these propositions was not tested in this study (it is doubtful that methodological tools are available for an empirical test). The second proved not to be the case; few of those interviewed wanted to lead segregated lives. This preference may, of course, change in the future, but that possibility is not relevant here, for apart from the question of preference it seems that structural forces and attitudes prevent people from even exposing themselves to discrimination. In addition, our evidence suggests strongly that many people who do expose themselves to discrimination fail to utilize the law, and that those who do are unrepresentative. Forces similar to those observed in the welfare situation inhibit the utilization of the law and access to bureaucracy—lack of opportunity, lack of knowledge of the law (or recognition that the law may have been violated), lack of knowledge of channels for complaint, and negative attitudes toward law and bureaucracy. It seems again that all of these obstacles to access are more prevalent in low-status groups.

Up to this point we have been considering obstacles to the use of law that relies for its utilization upon individuals. The next chapter will examine the situation where the onus for initiating the law appears to be placed upon the bureaucracy itself. The question is whether this variety in responsibility for initiation will overcome the obstacles we have seen.

Law and Bureaucracy

Notes

1. *Mass. Acts of 1946*, c. 368. For a comprehensive study of the MCAD's early history and of the role of antidiscrimination law in Boston from 1959 to 1961, see L. Mayhew, *Law and Equal Opportunity* (1968). The present study will not, unless necessary, repeat what has been said there. It will, however, draw on the work that has been done in the hope that continuous study over time might add to our knowledge of the limits and possibilities of antidiscrimination law. For my review of Mayhew's book, see 83 *Harv. L. Rev.* 283 (1969).

2. Prohibiting discrimination in public housing projects, *Mass. Acts of 1950*, c. 697; on the grounds of age, *Mass. Acts of 1956*, c. 426; in educational institutions, *Mass. Acts of 1956*, c. 334; in publicly assisted housing, *Mass. Acts of 1957*, c. 426; in private housing, *Mass. Acts of 1959*, c. 239 (the constitutionality of which was upheld in MCAD v. Colangelo, 344 Mass. 387, 182 N.E. 2d. 595 (1962); in the granting of mortgage loans, *Mass. Acts of 1960*, c. 163; in the sale of commercial space, *Mass. Acts of 1965*, c. 213; and on the grounds of sex in employment, *Mass. Acts of 1965*, c. 397.

3. By *Mass. Acts of 1950*, c. 479.

4. Two commissioners manned the Boston office, one the Springfield office. The chairman divided his time between the two. At public hearings three commissioners sit at whichever office is handling the case.

5. *Mass. Gen. Laws*, c. 151B, s. 3 (1965).

6. Former Chairman Mahoney informed one author that "the initiation of enforcement proceedings is inconsistent with the commission's function of adjusting complaints through conciliation." J. Witherspoon, "Civil Rights Policy in the Federal System: Proposals for a Better Use of the Administrative Process," 74 *Yale L.J.* 1117, 1192 (1965).

7. Other than those covering advertisements and application forms, three complaints alleging housing discrimination and seven complaints alleging discrimination in employment were issued. These were all against employment agencies which allegedly refused to process job orders for blacks, and were settled informally.

8. See note 44, *infra*.

9. See note 45, *infra*.

10. Elapsed time between the alleged unlawful discriminatory conduct and the filing of the complaint varied widely. The mean time for filing housing complaints was 4.4 days. One-third of all housing complaints were filed within one day of discrimination, one-half within four days, and 55 of the 63 cases, within one week. The mean time between the alleged discrimination and the filing of employment complaints was 11.97 days. Half the employment cases were filed within one week of the alleged discrimination.

11. There are six field representatives in the Boston MCAD office. Each is a licensed notary public.

12. Concerning the complainant's education, income, work record, size of family, and so forth.

13. Forty percent of housing complaints were investigated within 24 hours of filing, and over half within 48 hours. The mean time between the filing of the complaint and investigation was 3.53 days for housing cases and 3.38 days for employment cases. One-third of the employment investigations were conducted within 24 hours of the complaint.

14. In only two of the cases was a subpoena necessary to compel a respondent to disclose his records.

15. Mayhew, *op. cit.*, c. VII, contends that the commission was concerned only with the "reasonableness" of the qualification demanded from the complainant, and not with "equal treatment"—i.e., a concern to investigate whether the same qualifications were demanded from other individuals with whom the respondent had similar dealings. In 1965, however, the field representatives took care to ascertain "equal" and "reasonable" treatment. What the MCAD did not seek to ascertain, however, was whether qualifications that would be "reasonable" for the majority of white applicants were possible devices to discriminate against blacks as a group. For example, the qualification of a small family or a male head of household, in housing, or the passing of a "culturally biased" intelligence test in employment. See Myart v. Motorola, Inc., 9 *Race Rel. L. R.* 1911 (1964), and J. Kaplan, "Equal Justice in an Unequal World; Equality for the Negro—The Problem of Special Treatment," 61 *N. W. L. Rev.* 363 (1966).

16. In a public hearing of one case the commission admitted evidence from the investigating commissioner of certain statements made by the respondent during the course of such a conference and held that these statements were not part of the nonadmissible endeavors toward conciliation.

17. See Chapter 6.

18. *Mass. Gen. Laws*, c. 151B, §5 (1965). After a finding of probable cause the commission has power to apply for an injunction to restrain the disposal of the property or employment in question. Fifteen of these applications were drawn up in 1965 (14 for housing, 1 for employment); many of these were settled out of court.

19. See Chapter 6.

20. The main reason for this was that two of the three commissioners would not order any affirmative action to be taken by the respondents, thus nothing positive could be reported. Further, the attorney general ruled in 1965 that firms may not keep racial records, for fear that they might set a quota on the number of blacks hired. *MCAD Annual Report*, at 16 (1965).

21. The MCAD chairman considers that such a decree, which may be enforced directly in the courts, is "harsh." A formal consent

agreement could be enforced as a contract between the parties, but such a technique would probably be "limited by judicial reluctance to order specific performance of personal-service contracts." M. Bamberger and N. Lewin, "Note," 74 *Harv. L. Rev.* 526, 546 (1961). And see H. Spitz, "Tailoring the Techniques to Eliminate and Prevent Employment Discrimination," 14 *Buffalo L. Rev.* 79 (1964).

22. Only 22 such hearings were held from 1946 to 1965. Only 2 were held prior to 1960.

23. *Mass. Gen. Laws*, c. 151B, s 5.

24. R. Girard and L. Jaffe, "Some General Observations on Administration of State Fair Employment Practice Laws," 14 *Buffalo L.R.* 114, 115 (1964).

25. Mayhew, *op. cit.* at 159.

26. Mayhew raises briefly the possibility that rates of complaint may not coincide with incidence of complaint, but concludes that the two probably are coincidental. *Ibid.*, at 157-158.

27. Massachusetts Advisory Committee to the U. S. Commission on Civil Rights, *Report on Massachusetts: Housing in Boston*, Appendix 1, *Annual Report, Fair Housing Inc.*, *April 1962-March 1963*, at 66 (1963). In employment, too, it seems that less discrimination takes place against black professionals (although they are underrepresented relative to whites in this occupational category) than might take place against black sales or operative workers—work categories where blacks are overrepresented relative to whites, but where employers might set quotas on the numbers of blacks employed.

28. Seventeen percent of the complaints laid in 1959/1960 alleged discrimination in segregated black areas. Mayhew, *op. cit.*, at 172.

29. *U.S. Census of Population, op. cit.*

30. *Ibid.*

31. See the methodological note in the Introduction.

32. *The Middle-Income Negro Faces Urban Renewal*, Brandeis University, at 22 (1964).

33. T. Pettigrew, Metropolitan Planning Council of the Commonwealth of Massachusetts, "Metropolitan Boston's Race Problem in Perspective" in *Social Structure and Human Problems in the Boston Metropolitan Area*, at 42 (1965).

34. In order to make this response more action-oriented, the distinction was made between persons who planned to move in the near future. Of blacks who planned to move, 20.8% preferred an all-black area (compared with 9.5% of those who did not plan to move).

35. See J. Kaplan, "Equal Justice in an Unequal World: Equality for the Negro—The Problem of Special Treatment," 61 *N. W. L. Rev.* 363 (1966).

36. Mayhew, *op. cit.*, at 67, and chapt. 3.

37. J. Kain, *The Effect of the Ghetto on the Distribution and Level of Non-White Employment in Urban Areas (1965).*

38. Pettigrew, "Metropolitan Boston's Race Problem in Perspective." *op. cit.*, at 44.

39. K. Clark, "Black and White: The Ghetto Inside," *Boston*, October 1965, 21, at 26.

40. A study in 1948 of the influence of discrimination upon Jews in New York identified the "repression-type" who would refuse consciously to recognize that any discrimination existed in the community, and the "suppression-type" who would erect a psychological defence mechanism and refuse to recognize that *he* would be subjected to discriminatory treatment. G. Saenger and N. Gordon, "The Influence of Discrimination on Minority Group Members in its Relations to Attempts to Combat Discrimination," 31 *J. of Soc. Psychology* 95 (1950).

41. Interview with Field Representative C.

42. Of those with an education below high school, only 26% knew of the MCAD, compared with 38% of high school and 63% of college graduates. Of those under 25 years of age, only 20% knew of the MCAD, compared with about 64% of those over that age.

43. This figure does not include 4 cases that went to public hearing. It does include cases that were discontinued or where lack of jurisdiction was found. During 1965, 102 complaints were filed at the Boston office, and 24 at the Springfield office. Seventy-one of the 85 cases closed were also filed in 1965. The 85 cases were filed by 78 complainants against 80 respondents. Seventy complaints alleged refusal to rent a property; 9, refusal to sell; 1, refusal to build; 1, discriminatory eviction; 1, discriminatory conditions; and 1, failure to grant a mortgage. Thirty-five of the 85 were laid against real estate brokers, 50 against individuals.

44. This figure lists as 1 complaint cases laid by 20 complainants and listed by the MCAD as 20 of the 71 complaints filed during the year at the Boston office; 23 were filed at the Springfield office. In addition, the MCAD processed 248 cases alleging discriminatory advertising or application forms in 1965, but most of these alleged discrimination on the ground of age. Thirty-nine of the 45 complaints were laid in 1965. The complaints were laid by 43 complainants against 43 respondents. Sixteen alleged refusal to hire; 10, refusal to refer; 2, discriminatory conditions; 14, discriminatory discharge; 1, discriminatory transfer.

45. Some complainants may simply have been testing for discrimination and never intended use of the offer.

46. The "strategic" success of the complaint will be discussed below.

47. The responses also varied according to which commissioner handled the complainant's case. This will be considered in Chapter 6.

48. "for most people, wearing their dark skin color is like living with a chronic disease. One learns to 'take it' and not let it unduly cramp one's style of life." St. C. Drake and H. Cayton, *Black Metropolis*, vol. 2, at XXVI (1962).

49. The American Jewish Congress suggested reasons why Jewish complainants in 1953 would be reluctant to file a complaint with the

MCAD against an employer: "Sometimes they fear such action may hurt their chances with other employers. Sometimes they have secured other jobs speedily and put aside their resentment. Sometimes they are frightened at the prospect of becoming involved themselves and involving others in legal proceedings." "Confidential Memorandum on the MCAD," at 4 (1953).

50. L. Zeitz, "Survey of Negro Attitudes to Law," 19 *Rutgers L. Rev.* 288 (1965).

51. Five of 36.

52. Of the five who claimed that they would not use the MCAD, three thought that "you can't change people's feelings"; one did not want to "take his troubles on the street," and one would consider prayer a more appropriate course of action.

53. Of those with a college education, 54.5% (12) favored education, compared with 73.2% (41) of those who had not attended high school. Of white-collar workers, 56.2% (18) favored education, compared with 85.3% (29) of blue-collar workers.

4

Officially Initiated Access: Citizen Participation in Urban Renewal

Under the Federal Housing Act of 1954, a local public agency in charge of urban redevelopment must, in order for its proposals to qualify for federal approval as a "workable program," satisfy the requirement of "citizen participation" in the planning of the proposal.[1]

On its face, the requirement of "citizen participation" would seem to suggest that the urban renewal agency is itself charged with initiating access of the persons who will be affected by its operations. This might avoid some of the obstacles to individually initiated access to law or bureaucracy. The planning process provides an example of an administrative task that is functionally distinct from those considered thus far.

This chapter examines the operations of the Boston Redevelopment Authority (BRA). A BRA project in the Madison Park area of Boston's predominantly black Roxbury will be analyzed and supplemented by the attitudes of about half of the residents remaining in the area in mid-1968.

ORGANIZATIONAL STRUCTURE

The 1949 Housing Act[2] established the concept of urban redevelopment in the United States. Its goals were proclaimed as the "feasible ones" of a "decent home and a suitable living environment for every American family, thus contributing to the development and the redevelopment of communities and the advancement of the growth, wealth, and security of the Nation."[3] The act aimed at encouraging local governments to reverse the spread of "urban blight" in residential areas; and to create "well planned, integrated, residential neighborhoods."[4] The incentive for the 1949 legislation grew out of concern for what was considered a "deterioration"[5] of local neighborhoods and the subsequent reduction in the taxable base of these areas, as well as for the increased cost of services such as low-income housing, which the municipalities were expected to provide. Private enterprise could not be depended upon to rebuild the center cities. The act thus provided for substantial federal aid to local public agencies authorized by state enabling legislation to undertake "redevelopment."[6]

The program is administered between Washington and the local city hall, with the regional office acting as monitor and process point. The program is instigated, however, entirely at the local level, under standards that are inevitably vague, because the act must apply to thousands of communities, each with differing conditions. As Greer has said, "At the highest level of generality, the Housing Act requires planning."[7]

The "redevelopment" approach of the 1949 Act had been preceded by two different approaches. The 1934 Housing Act[8] created the Federal Housing Authority with the primary purpose of financing loans by approved agencies for the purchase, construction, repair, and improvement of homes. The 1937 Act[9] was directed largely to the elimination of "slums"—areas considered "unsafe," "insanitary," or "contagious"—and the building of subsidized housing in their place. Dissatisfaction with the results of these acts provoked the search for new methods.

The first few years of implementation of the 1949 act gave rise to further dissatisfaction: Individuals were displaced by projects in a time of housing shortage, and "blight" seemed to be outpacing "redevelopment." The 1954 Housing Act[10] therefore introduced a major innovation: a departure from the old "slum clearance" approach and a new emphasis on conservation and rehabilitation of existing housing. The chief innovation of the 1954 act was the listing of seven requirements for a "workable program"[11] necessary for federal approval.

State enabling legislation differs according to the nature, functions, and powers of the local public agency authorized to carry out renewal. Until it was abolished in 1960, a 9-member volunteer planning board, appointed by the mayor and assisted by a staff of about 45, coordinated renewal and redevelopment projects in Boston.[12] In 1957 the Boston Redevelopment Authority (BRA) was created from a division in the Boston Housing Authority.[13] Its function was, in theory, to execute urban renewal projects delineated by the planning board in accordance with the city's comprehensive development plan drawn up in 1950.[14] In practice the BRA performed the task of "real estate speculation"[15] and "went about the business of picking off prime real estate packages scattered throughout the city."[16] Up to 1959 urban renewal in Boston typified the "bulldozer" approach, clearing cohesive and vital neighborhoods that were wrongly perceived to be slums and substituting luxury apartments in their place. The urban renewal project in Boston's West End constitutes perhaps the clearest example of such an approach and has been vividly described by Herbert Gans in *The Urban Villagers*.[17]

In 1959 John Collins was elected mayor of Boston on a program pledging the improved coordination, control, and rationalization of urban planning.[18] One of Collins' first acts in office was to appoint Edward J. Logue, then in charge of New Haven's urban renewal program, as consultant. Logue advised the restructuring of urban planning, in a manner that would give him full control over the new machinery himself. Collins succeeded in abolishing the old planning board and making the BRA the local public agency in charge of both planning and executing federally assisted urban renewal projects. Logue was appointed head of the BRA as well as head of the Mayor's Office of Development. As development administrator he was thus in full control of all city planning in Boston.[19]

Drawing on the support of Boston business interests and that of Mayor Collins and demonstrating his proven capacity for obtaining federal funds, Logue constructed a large and powerful agency, which devised plans for a "90 Million Dollar Development Program for Boston,"[20] under the slogan "Planning with People."[21]

The enabling legislation gives the BRA authority to prepare and execute an urban renewal plan. After a survey of the area the agency will then draw up a plan which may be put to a public hearing after due notice.[22] After the public hearing, which is held before the BRA, the proposals will be submitted to the city council which will hold a further public hearing.[23] Thereafter the plan will be submitted to the Department of Housing and Urban Development, which will determine whether it meets with statutory standards.[24]

From the date of the passing of the 1949 Act to the present time, the courts have given little assistance to an individual challenging an urban renewal agency's actions.[25] The Massachusetts act gives an individual the right to petition the courts within thirty days of the approval of a project by the BRA in order "to correct errors of law" in the plan.[26] Legal remedies have rarely been forthcoming, however; the issue upon which the cases turn has usually been framed in terms of whether a "public use or purpose" exists to justify the use of land acquisition. The U.S. Supreme Court in the case of *Berman* v. *Parker* laid down the rationale for limited use of judicial review:

Subject to specific constitutional limitations, when the legislature has spoken, the public interest has been declared in terms well-nigh conclusive. In such cases the legislature, not the judiciary, is the main guardian of the public need to be served by social legislation. . . . The role of the judiciary in determining whether that power is being exercised for a public purpose is an extremely narrow one.[27]

The Massachusetts cases have expressed similar reasoning. The courts have been content to rely upon the discretion of the agency to determine the public need where its actions have been "reasonable." In *Despatchers Cafe* v. *Somerville Housing Authority* the court stated that "if there is any room for discretion, the judgment of the Board must prevail," and was careful not to "hamper public officials" in the performance of duties necessary to public welfare.[28] An individual would thus be able to restrain the BRA's actions only where those actions had been "capricious," "arbitrary," and an "abuse of discretion." As a recent case has stated, "courts are not authorized to second guess the authorities."[29]

The obligation of the BRA or city council to take note of objections voiced at a public hearing is similarly limited because these hearings do not take the form of a "trial," but of "argument."[30] The Massachusetts Supreme Judicial Court has recently held that the public hearing is "legislative" in nature; thus no legal remedy can be claimed on the basis of the record of the hearing.[31]

CITIZEN PARTICIPATION IN URBAN RENEWAL

In order to carry out a "workable program" for urban renewal, the local public agency must provide for "citizen participation."[32] Because neither the 1954 Housing Act nor its amendments or regulations detail the administrative structure required for citizen participation, the local public agency possesses discretion to determine its extent or form.[33]

It should be stressed, therefore, that a variety of alternative mechanisms for obtaining citizen participation might be employed. Different agencies might have differing interpretations, first of whom among the citizen population should be selected for participation, and second of the kind and extent of participatory mechanisms to use. These choices will be made on the basis of the perceived purposes of citizen participation. Before considering the mechanisms employed in Boston, these alternatives will be examined. We shall then be able to evaluate the BRA's approach.

The Purpose of Citizen Participation

At its idealistic extreme the purpose of citizen participation is to achieve a vital democratic process founded on the premise that decision making should be kept responsive to the needs of widely representative groups. It attempts to avoid arbitrary action by central planners in disregard of the legitimate desires of the people they serve. The requirement of citizen participation in urban renewal is thus a way of offsetting the monopoly of policy-making power possessed by appointed officials and ensuring their responsiveness to plural interests.[34]

Of course, how to achieve this purpose is one of the great local governmental problems of our time, when the urban environment is crowded with individuals with disparate interests competing for recognition. The issues to be determined, on the other hand, require an authoritative decision by those technically competent to comprehend their complexities and wise enough to glean the public interest or to mediate its emergence.

The history of citizen participation in urban renewal seems to be filled with cases of agencies paying symbolic or token service to the democratic ideal and using the requirement to promote the legitimacy of their own proposals or to offset spontaneous but disruptive participation of local protest groups.[35]

The New Haven Citizen's Action Commission, a citywide group of representatives who formed the citizen participating group when Edward Logue was development administrator in New Haven, was described by Dahl, through the words of

New Haven Mayor Lee, as comprising "the biggest set of muscles in New Haven."[36] He continued:

Except for a few trivial instances, the "muscles" never directly initiated, opposed, vetoed, or altered any proposals brought before them by the mayor and his development administrator.[37]

The members of the Citizen's Action Commission described their function as that of a "selling organization."[38] Dahl says that the endorsement of the commission

made the program appear nonpartisan, virtually nullified the effectiveness of partisan attacks, presented to the public an appearance of power and responsibility diffused among a representative group of community notables, and inhibited criticisms of even the most daring and ambitious parts of the program as "unrealistic" or "unbusinesslike." Indeed, by creating the CAC the Mayor virtually decapitated the opposition.[39]

In the long run, however, such cynical manipulation of the requirement of citizen participation may have harmed the legitimacy of urban renewal programs in particular, and of local government in general, especially in the perception of those most likely to be adversely affected by the programs—the poor and minority groups. Perhaps in consequence, citizen participation has recently undergone radical reinterpretation.

Citizen Participation and the OEO's Community Action Program

The contemporary connotation of citizen participation is very much colored by the requirement in the Economic Opportunity Act of "maximum feasible participation" of the poor.[40] The origin of the phrase has recently been the subject of debate and explanation.[41] Whether it is presently interpreted in accordance with the intention of one or all of its drafters, or whether it is within the scope of the original legislative purpose is not relevant for our present aims. What is relevant is that another rationale has arisen for citizen participation, which is bound to influence its interpretation under the "workable program" provision.

Under this interpretation citizen participation is seen as an end in itself to combat poverty. Not only will the involvement of poor citizens ensure institutional responsiveness, but, in addition, neighborhoods will be organized as a means to reduce apathy among the poor and as a form of sociotherapy to the community and participating individuals.[42] The Cahns make the point that

Participation is, in fact, the necessary concomitant of our faith in the dignity and worth of the individual. The denial of effective participation ... is a denial of the individual's own worth and a confirmation of his impotency and subserviency.[43]

A contemporary view of citizen participation thus considers the mobilization of the poor important in itself so that they may have the "satisfaction of performing civic duties"[44] as well as that of achieving political victories, and so that these satisfactions may, in consequence, provide an antidote for conditions of mind such as powerlessness, hopelessness, or alienation and ultimately bring about the rehabilitation of the dignity of the individual or community as well as that of structures in the area.

The Procedures of Citizen Participation

The three main purposes of citizen participation—to promote organizational responsiveness, the legitimacy of urban renewal, and sociotherapy to affected communities or individuals—all seem to be present in some degree in most contemporary explanations of the requirement.[45] But how is it to be structured? The question poses a problem in institutional design. At the least the structure could provide selected interest groups with institutionalized access to the local public agency. At most it could provide every community with the power to veto the agency's proposals.

The "citizen" population selected to participate in either scheme could include residents of the proposed renewal area or residents of the entire city. In the former case the population with whom the agency intends to "participate" could include every individual, representatives of neighborhood organizations, interests, or institutions, ad hoc protest groups, or a number of individuals selected because of their prominence or influence. Similarly, where the appropriate population is citywide, it could include every individual, citywide representatives, or selected individuals.[46]

The requirement of "participation" could be satisfied by the agency demonstrating any of the following:

1. *Information dissemination.* The agency could show the lowest order of participation where the contents of the proposed plan, and any other information relating to the program, had been conveyed to the selected citizen population in the affected area. The citizens selected might be every individual in the area or only community representatives, who would then be assigned the function of communicating the information to individuals in the area.

2. *Agency availability.* At the next level of participation the agency could show that it not only had disseminated information but also had made itself available to receive suggestions or criticism from the citizens. Here the agency might open a site office in the area, with a staff available to receive any resident. Alternatively, the agency might make itself available to community or citywide representatives alone, from whom it would hear suggestions or objections to its proposals.

3. *Agency consultation.* Here the agency could show that it had solicited the opinions of the citizens for the purpose of identifying their needs. This involves more than passive availability and could be carried out by a research survey, by periodic advertised walks through the area for the purpose of discovering neighborhood opinion, by placing neighborhood representatives on an advisory board, or by holding public meetings.

In order for citizen participation to be more than symbolic or token,[47] the agency must show that through its availability or communications it had, in fact, adopted suggestions and made appropriate changes, or at least had given genuine consideration to advice that was contrary to its own plan. In other words, it should be amenable to influence through citizen participation. Some agencies might not wish to rely on the spontaneous expression of citizen grievances and instead might take steps to articulate them through encouragement of the organization of neighborhood groups, through the mobilization of the community, or through the training of community leadership.

4. *Citizen approval.* The most complete level of participation exists where the agency could show that its proposals received the support of the selected citizen population. This support could be demonstrated by means of a referendum or an opinion poll. Similarly, the support of area representatives could be demonstrated through the vote of a committee of representatives or the expression of their support at a public hearing. This would amount to giving the citizens a veto over agency proposals.

It should be stressed that these categories of participation are simplifications and that actual techniques might be somewhere between two of them.[48] For instance, power could be shared between a citizen representative committee and the agency, thus giving citizens considerable say, but falling short of giving them a veto. In addition, these techniques are not mutually exclusive. They could be combined, and different techniques might be employed with different sections of the citizen population. For example, the agency could make itself available to all the individuals in the area and carry on consultations with, or obtain the approval of, the citywide representatives alone.

The purpose of the simplification is to draw a distinction between degrees of participation in order to better understand the alternatives, and to allow us some standard by which to evaluate the requirements and procedures of HUD and the BRA.

HUD Requirements

The HUD publication pertaining to citizen participation issued at the time of this study stated:

Experience has demonstrated that effective citizen participation over the extended period necessary to carry out a successful Workable Program is based on an active citizen advisory committee. This is communitywide and representative in scope, officially designated by the mayor and/or council, in accordance with local custom.[49]

The Department defined "communitywide" as including

a cross-section of all elements in the community. It should not be confined to any one segment of the population. It should include persons from all the principal neighborhoods.[50]

According to these federal requirements, therefore, the appropriate citizen population was to include representatives from citywide as well as neighborhood organizations, institutions, and interests.

The form of participation envisaged was the use of the citizens advisory committee as a two-way communications link, bringing information to the agency (agency consultation) and from the agency to the affected community (information dissemination).[51]

Later HUD requirements appeared to recognize the symbolically reassuring nature of some mechanisms of citizen participation, stating that

voting, attendance at meetings, letters to Congressmen are frequently ineffective in dealing with the immediate problems raised by increasingly large and complex programs having direct impact on people's lives.[52]

In order to alter this situation, the guidelines propose that "new communitywide advisory committees"[53] be established, embracing all major interests including the poor and members of minority groups, or that new special purpose groups be set up and coordination encouraged with existing advisory committees, such as those set up under the Model Cities program.[54] It is further suggested that citizen committees and neighborhood groups be given specific functions such as holding public hearings, preparing comments on workable program applications, conducting interviews and surveys of neighborhood residents, and establishing information centers. It is also suggested that specific methods be developed to ensure the representativeness of advisory committees (such as including equal proportions from private neighborhood groups, government-program-connected advisory groups, and civic groups). The guidelines recommend the establishment of a planning group "to help develop new ideas and techniques for generating greater involvement among poor and disadvantaged groups."[55]

These guidelines thus go some way toward the establishment of a representative body of citizens with positive organizational tasks enabling it to bring information about citizen needs to the agency. They fall short, however, of proposing either any specific participatory mechanisms to ensure agency amenability to community desires or any community veto over official proposals.

In order to appreciate the practical problems involved in one urban renewal project, the BRA's Madison Park area project will be considered.

URBAN RENEWAL IN ACTION: MADISON PARK[56]

In 1962 the Harvard University Graduate School of Education, under contract with the city of Boston, undertook a survey and made recommendations concerning the city's school-building needs. The recommendations were endorsed by the mayor, the school committee, and BRA, all collaborators in the project. The keystone recommendation was a proposal for a new high school to replace the present English High School building and to improve and expand the programs it offered. The school would accommodate 5000 students and would be constructed in a campus style.

The Boston School Committee considered various sites for the new school, and the choice eventually narrowed to two alternatives: Franklin Park or the Madison Park area in Lower Roxbury. The school committee initially objected to the Madison Park site on the grounds that it was a low-income, predominantly black area, but because the Franklin Park site was owned by the Commonwealth of Massachusetts, an act of the legislature was required for the city to gain possession of it. The school committee proposed such legislation; it was passed in the teeth of strong opposition from the liberal community and black leaders who favored the Madison Park site as an opportunity to upgrade the area and to ensure a racially balanced school. The governor vetoed the legislation.

In February 1966, after four years of political wrangling, the school committee narrowly reversed itself in favor of the Madison Park site but stated that 60 acres should be allotted to the school. The initial proposals had recommended 30 acres. The Madison Park area contains 57 acres, and thus it would all be allotted to the school.

The Madison Park area is probably the most deteriorated section of Boston. Much of it is characterized by crumbling, deserted structures and vacant lots. Within its confines are some light industry and a high percentage of low-income housing, about 30 percent old owner-occupied houses. At the beginning of 1966 the area comprised approximately 400 households;[57] about one-third appear to have since moved out,[58] contributing further to the area's deserted atmosphere.

Although approximately one-third of the households are on welfare, an almost equal percentage earn over $6000 per year. Like other parts of Roxbury, Madison Park is an area of comparatively recent black influx and white outflow.[59]

About 60 percent of the households are black; 40 percent white. Although the mean age of the area is 52.2, the whites are on average older than the blacks.[60] Because of this age difference about 42 percent of the white households receive annual incomes under $3000, compared with 21.2 percent of the black households.

After a four-year delay the head of the BRA, Edward J. Logue, was eager to proceed with the project and scheduled a public hearing before the BRA for July 25, 1966, in order to decide the question of early acquisition of the sixty acres where the school would be built.[61] The project director had made no effort to consult with the people of the area or to advertise his availability for two reasons: First, he thought that there was no point in consulting with people who would all be moved out of the area; and second, he "didn't think that they were particularly the people to plan a high school with."[62]

Just prior to the hearing, an ad hoc organization known as the Lower Roxbury Community Committee on Urban Renewal (LRCC) was formed in order to campaign for on-site housing to be included in the urban renewal plan. The formation of the LRCC was the culmination of the concern of the heads of two settlement houses and a church council of the area that low-income housing be available in Madison Park. The LRCC's first task was to circulate a petition which was presented to the BRA and recommended that early land acquisition be postponed until the community could become fully involved in the planning. The petition also requested that 25 of the 60 acres of the site be used for housing and community facilities for the householders who would be displaced and wished to remain in the area. Logue insisted on the necessity of the school as the "key to the Boston school construction program"[63] and refused to halt arrangements for the hearing.

On the day of the hearing the LRCC announced at a press conference that it had entered into a contract with Urban Planning Aid, Inc., a group of architects, planners, sociologists, and other professionals who would represent the LRCC in its dealings with the BRA. Urban Planning Aid is a nonprofit corporation staffed largely by young Harvard, MIT, and Brandeis University professors organized to serve as "advocate planners," giving "professional guidance"[64] to local low-income communities and representing them before public agencies as a lawyer would his client.

The public hearing was held as scheduled.[65] More than 700 residents filled the hall of a local school. There were 43 speakers representing 13 neighborhood organizations and 5 churches, 7 unaffiliated residents, 3 political representatives of the area, 3 public officials, a spokesman for the Harvard School of Education, 2 representatives of the NAACP, the chairman of the Greater Boston Chamber of Commerce, and 5 speakers from other areas in Boston.

The entire meeting was united on the school issue. It cut across all differences and successfully provoked unanimous approval for the project as a whole. Because the question put to the meeting required a yes or no vote and the concept of the school received unanimous approval, alternative suggestions were all expressed in the form of qualified approval. The main qualification, expressed by 6 of the 13 neighborhood organizations, was on the question of low-income housing. The LRCC, through three spokesmen, all residents of the area, put forward an alternative plan.[66] Its central proposal was that new low- and moderate-income housing be built on at least 25 acres of land allocated to the project area. The LRCC also expressed disappointment at the lack of citizen participation and requested a voice in the future planning process. Other demands of the LRCC included housing for the elderly, scattered-site public housing, a program of rehabilitation of existing structures, a phased relocation project, and a scheme whereby displaced businessmen would be given preference in the allocation of space in the new shopping centers.

Three of the five church representatives supported the demand for low-income housing, two of them explicitly on the grounds that they would otherwise lose their congregations. The two representatives of the NAACP made no mention of housing but expressed support for the school because it would be racially balanced. Two of the seven residents who spoke requested additional housing in the area, and one approved the project because it would enable her to receive compensation and leave the area.

About two months later Logue presented a memorandum to the BRA.[67] He stated that the public hearing had indicated overwhelming support for the school and examined four reservations expressed at the meeting. First, the acreage requested by the School Committee was excessive: Logue recommended that the BRA advise the Public Facilities Department, which would have power to determine the acreage of all schools,[69] that the project acquire only as much land as was "required for the proper development of the school." Second, the question of low- and moderate-income housing: Logue stated that his personal preference "goes very strongly against putting housing of any type in this location," because existing housing would be available and adequate for relocation and that there was "a serious risk of creating a ghetto condition." The remaining two objections, relating to the early land acquisition and the BRA's policy of "planning with people," led Logue to reaffirm his policy of "consultation with the community about all measures which are planned for the community, and seeking to learn from the community its preferences, and, insofar as possible, to formulate its plans so as to accommodate community needs and preferences." Nevertheless, Logue could not see "any reason in public policy or common sense" for abandoning the early land acquisition plan.[69]

During late September and early October 1966, the project director consulted with some of the community organizations, and on October 11 Logue indicated to the BRA that these discussions "indicate a clear commitment by the Authority," and in view of the residents' "legitimate concerns" recommended that the BRA allocate a minimum of 15 acres of land for the construction of between 400 and 600 units of new moderate- and low-income housing.[70] A month later the Public Facilities Department ruled that 35 acres would be sufficient for the school. With 15 acres now available, the BRA revised its initial plan in order to provide for the housing.

The Hearing Before the City Council[71]

On November 16, 1966, the revised plan was considered by the Boston City Council's Committee on Urban Renewal. Logue stated that the city stood to gain financially if the school were built under the renewal program and said that the project director has "met repeatedly with the members of the Lower Roxbury community and others interested and concerned in an effort to work out a satisfactory solution which takes into account the interests of the people in this particular neighborhood as well as the interests of the city as a whole."[72]

Objections were made to the new plan. The LRCC chairman stated that it was "neither specific enough or firm enough to guarantee what the community needs; for example, there is no statement on prices of housing units or their location in the staging of their construction."[73] Gordon Fellman, an assistant professor of sociology at Brandeis University, represented the LRCC on behalf of Urban Planning Aid and repeated the desire for a firm commitment. He stated that interviews carried out by the LRCC with the help of his organization showed that about 70 percent of the 400 families to be displaced wanted to remain in the neighborhood,[74] and he requested that the BRA guarantee 400 units of which 60 percent should rent for between $45 and $75 per month; the remaining 40 percent to range between $75 and $115, with 30 percent ownership in each category. Finally, Fellman demanded the "staging" of all relocation.[75]

Support for the BRA's plan came from the state representatives of the area, the chairman of the NAACP Educational Committee, the Ministers Interdenominational Alliance (comprising forty clergymen), and the superintendent of Boston schools. Opposition came from the head of an area settlement house who said that the BRA was using the school as "blackmail" to gain support for the entire project.[76]

The afternoon of November 18, 1966, turned out to be a stormy session of the council. Logue stated that he was prepared to work out an "acceptable commitment" to ensure low- and moderate-rental housing on the 15-acre site not needed for the school. But whereas he was prepared to enter into an agreement with the "residents of the area," he refused to meet with the advocate planners whom he dubbed "academic amateurs from across the river . . . out to have a little fun."[77] He insisted that "This isn't a plaything, a tinker-toy for MIT" and that he intended "to resolve this with . . . the people of the area."[78]

Stung by these charges, which had received wide publicity, the LRCC chairman presented to the next meeting of the city council committee a petition with the names of 300 Madison Park residents who claimed to be represented by the LRCC. Urban Planning Aid presented statements from various university professors lauding the group as "responsible professionals." But Logue reiterated that he would discuss the matter only with the LRCC chairman and other residents of the area.[79]

During the next week the BRA held two private negotiation sessions with LRCC members. The meeting was also attended by two advocate planners, who simply walked into the conference after being excluded by BRA staff members. Logue agreed to accept the LRCC's demands on low-income housing with three compromises: The first eliminated the LRCC's demand for veto power over subsequent plans; the second eliminated a proposed stipulation that residents of the area be contracted as developers of the new housing; and the third eliminated the specific rental schedule proposed. Logue said that the BRA would approve a memorandum embodying this compromise as soon as it was accepted by members of LRCC and that he would ask Mayor Collins to sign it.[80]

On the evening of December 1, 1966, forty members of the LRCC met to consider the compromise memorandum and voted unanimously to attach five stipulations to it: inclusion of LRCC veto power; specification of the precise amount of low-income housing in the proposed 400 units; the right to review the relocation procedure; specification of the number of moderate-income housing units and the terms of ownership; and provision for specific landscaping to shield the area from proposed new expressways alongside the site.[81]

At a later meeting between the LRCC and the BRA, however, the LRCC backed down from its stipulations and accepted the compromise memorandum.[82] Logue considered that the recent formation of the LRCC precluded granting it veto power but offered to reconsider this issue after a few months. Urban Planning Aid claimed that "this memorandum marks the first time that a community-based organization representing both low- and middle-income families has organized on its own and won an important, if incomplete, part in the planning process."[83]

Shortly afterwards Logue left the BRA. During the next three years the application for early land acquisition remained pending, and federal approval had not been granted. Meanwhile, Madison Park became more and more desolate, and more and more residents, uncertain about the future of the area, moved out.

The LRCC remained active. It formed itself into a nonprofit corporation and organized to construct the proposed housing. After a good deal of wrangling, the LRCC finally wrought from the BRA most of the concessions it had been seeking. John Sharratt, an architect hired by the LRCC, had designed the housing (283 low-density units, combining

90 town houses and housing for the elderly; for about one-fourth, rents would be geared to income). The BRA agreed that residents would be employed in housing management, and arrangements were worked out for the LRCC to obtain eventual ownership.

How do we assess the Madison Park experience? In some respects it could be said that the LRCC, despite their earlier setbacks, achieved a spectacular victory in being granted almost complete control of the planning, construction, and management of the housing (assuming all the necessary approvals and finances in the future). On the other hand, the vast majority of Madison Park residents left the area, directly because of the blight induced by the urban renewal designation and the uncertainty and delay.

The LRCC victory was clear. What is less clear is the extent of citizen participation in the drafting of the plan. This question will now be examined.

The Extent of Citizen Participation

From its actions in Madison Park it seems that the BRA was careful to pay attention to *pro forma* manifestations of citizen participation, particularly through the device of the public hearing. Clearly, however, these hearings were no more than acts of symbolic or token reassurance[84] designed to satisfy the democratic rules of the game. The project director himself felt strongly that Madison Park residents were not the people with whom to plan a high school. The same Project Director addressed another meeting:

The question was asked, "How much do you consider the opinion of

the residents of the area?" The answer was "We try to convince the important people in the area that they support the project."
However, urban renewal, it seems, is tempered somewhat by public opinion. "We are more hesitant in the precincts Mayor Collins didn't carry," Mr. Stainton explained.[85]

The BRA thus began the Madison Park project with the view that citizen participation was primarily a method of promoting the legitimacy of urban renewal and of gaining public support for a project. Logue's strategy had not changed from the one he employed in New Haven. In the end, however, Logue acceded to most of the LRCC's demands, and it seems probable now that the LRCC's role in the planning of the scheme had been almost total, and that their role in the building and running of the scheme is likely to be considerable. The reason for the BRA's concessions will be analyzed later. For the moment it is sufficient to suggest that their power became increasingly eroded due to setbacks in other areas of Boston.

The question we are asking now, however, is, What was the extent of citizen participation in Madison Park? Both the BRA and the LRCC claimed to represent the views of the residents, and it would seem that after the publicity and public hearings most residents would have been involved in participation. The tabulations below, however, show that a large proportion of the residents interviewed claimed both a lack of opportunity to participate in the BRA's planning and a lack of knowledge of the plan.

Tables 4.1 and 4.2 show that over half of the sample claimed that the BRA had done nothing to communicate the contents of the plan to them, and 63 percent said that the BRA had not sought their views of the plan.

This apparently low extent of consultation with or dissemination of information by the BRA to the residents

Table 4.1*   Residents' Knowledge of Means of Participation:
"Did the BRA do anything to let you know about the urban renewal plan for this area?"

	Percentage (N=103)
No	54%
Yes	
Public meeting	16
Personal solicitation	14
Letter	12
Told to move	3
Newspapers	1
Total	100%

*In this and other tables the number of respondents interviewed was 100 or close to it. Percentages will thus be employed, unless it is necessary to indicate the numbers.

Table 4.2   Response to: *"Did the BRA give you a chance to tell them about how you felt about the plan?"*

	Percentage (N=102)
No	63%
Yes	
Public meetings	30
Through the LRCC	3
Other	4
Total	100%

was further reflected in the residents' knowledge of the urban renewal plan. When asked if they knew whether they would be required by the urban renewal plan to move out of their homes, two-thirds of the sample did not know—a response indicating a high degree of ignorance on the part of individuals who were apparently informed by the BRA of the plan. When asked whether the plan provided for a citywide, racially mixed school, 42 percent of the sample were ignorant or uncertain of that fact.

Table 4.3 shows the response to a question seeking to ascertain the respondent's view of the best way to effect a change in an urban renewal plan he opposed. Almost a quarter would join existing organizations or work through existing institutions. Seventeen percent would initiate political action (such as petition, meeting, or demonstration), and 2 percent would approach a lawyer. Over half of the sample, however, were totally ignorant of what action to take. Of these, one-third did not know what action to take, and one in five was firm in their belief that nothing could be done.

Table 4.3   Best Way to Change an Urban Renewal Plan

Method	Percentage
Organizational participation	23%
Political initiative	17
Law	2
Don't know	32
Nothing can be done	21
Would not wish to effect changes	5
Total	100%

Eighty-five percent of those interviewed had, in fact, heard that the public hearing had taken place, but many clearly did not perceive the hearing as an opportunity to participate in the planning process. Only one-half of those who were aware of the public hearing attended.[86]

About one-half of the respondents were therefore ignorant both of the urban renewal plan for Madison Park and of the procedures for participation. Why was this so? The Madison Park area is cohesive in size and small in population, and surely the BRA could have informed the residents or elicited their views. Not all the blame, however, for the low degree of participation lies with the BRA. Factors that are endemic to urban poverty were at play. We have reviewed the conditions that inhibit participation that must be initiated by the individual. Similar limitations inhibit participation in the planning process when the onus of promoting that participation is placed upon the bureaucracy.

LIMITS TO CITIZEN PARTICIPATION IN URBAN RENEWAL

James Q. Wilson has written that the BRA's motto, Planning with People, "assumes on the part of the people involved a willingness and a capacity to engage in a collaborative search for the common good."[87] Various studies have indicated, however, that both willingness and capacity—at least in poor people—are absent.[88] Three BRA project directors stated that they had to "force" or "badger" citizen relocation or urban renewal committees to organize their own communities.[89] Interviews with Madison Park residents revealed two main obstacles to citizen participation in urban planning: a lack of involvement among a high proportion of the residents in neighborhood affairs generally, and a low assessment of their own political efficacy.

In 1918, an author wrote of a Chicago slum:

Behavior is individualized in the extreme. There is little or no public opinion. There is no common interest or cultural background. The greater part of the area is incapable of political action.[90]

The author considered that the transition from village to city life resulted in the breakup of a

120

common body of experience and tradition . . . unanimity of interest, sentiment, an attitude which can serve as a basis of collective action. Local groups do not act. They cannot act. Local life breaks down.[91]

Subsequent studies have suggested a more intricate network of relationships among urban dwellers than that author and members of the Chicago school of urban sociology perceived.[92] Nevertheless, a statement by the leader of a community group active in the BRA's South End urban renewal project (which was commenced just prior to the Madison Park project) indicates that the problem of low participation still exists. In a statement submitted to the BRA at a public hearing, the community leader said:

We endorse this plan because we feel that it strengthens the position of the Cathedral Housing Development in the community, but I should like this board to consider one point about which I am seriously concerned. I have stated that I represent the Cathedral Tenant's Association, but I cannot, in all honesty, say that our organization represents the people in our area. We have not more than twenty members participating, and there have been times when fewer than ten came to our meetings. Some seven hundred adults live in the Cathedral Project, which means that the views of only one in approximately forty people in our area are reflected in this plan.

It is my impression that this is true of many of the neighborhood organizations represented by the South End Urban Renewal Committee. I base this opinion on the reports of members of other associations, and on the appalling lack of knowledge about Urban Renewal and of the South End plan on the part of the average person on the street. Many people I have spoken to do not know that they have a neighborhood organization and have never heard of the South End Renewal Committee. The conclusion, then, is that the South End Urban Renewal Committee does not truly reflect the views and opinions of the people in the South End. Furthermore, it contains too many professional people . . . who exercise an influence on the committee's thinking and are given the privilege of a vote.

I do not know whether the fault lies with the BRA, which, it would seem, naively assumes that these neighborhood associations who have failed in their responsibility to get the message across, or with the people themselves, whom, I will admit, are apathetic and indifferent until something hits home. . . .[93]

This statement eloquently highlights many of the character-istic features of low-income communities: the low rate of involvement in community affairs and organizations, the low attendance at formal gatherings such as public meetings, the lack of knowledge of official action that might affect them, and a general apathy and indifference to public affairs, which allows better educated and professional people to assume key leadership roles.

The Madison Park area of Boston seems similarly to be characterized by lack of community involvement and lack of social contact among a high percentage of the residents, and particularly among those of a low educational status. Over a third of the sample stated that they were not interested in neighborhood affairs.[94] Despite the activity of the LRCC and other groups in the area, 65 percent could not name any community organization. Of those with less than eight years' schooling, over three out of four could not name a community organization,[95] compared with one-half of those who completed high school.[96] Eighty percent of the resi-dents had never attended any meeting of a neighborhood organization. Here again education proved significant: Only one in twenty[97] of those with less than eight years' education had ever attended a meeting, compared with two out of five of those who had completed high school.[98]

This lack of community involvement was not limited to the extent of participation in formal organizations. A full third of the Madison Park residents interviewed *never* met together socially with other people in the neighborhood, and another third socialized with their neighbors only a few times a year. Here too the lack of neighborhood socialization was significantly greater among the low-education population.[99]

These responses tally with various studies that find a low propensity to participate among low-status groups.[100] How-ever, few studies normally attempt to explain this lack of participation. Thus it might be concluded that lack of community interest or involvement is characteristic of lower-class status. Banfield argues that lower-class people are cognitively present-oriented—i.e. psychologically incapable of taking account of the future.[101] The interviews with Madison Park residents suggest that lack of participation is a consequence of a lower-class situation only insofar as people with little money have little residue of time and energy to expend on matters beyond the problems of daily living. It often is difficult for people with little education to articulate their wants and deal effectively with middle-class officials who speak in a "different language."[102] And lower-class people are apt to conclude, on the basis of past experience, that participation is not worth the time and effort.[103] The reasons given by those who failed to attend the Madison Park public hearings provide some indication of the causes of low participation.

Table 4.4   Reasons for Failure to Attend Public Hearing

Reason	Percentage	N
Inconvenient	57.1%	24
No use	14.3	6
Lack of interest	11.9	5
Other	16.7	7
Total	100.00%	42

Table 4.4 shows that over half failed to attend the hearing because it was inconvenient to do so. This response underlines an important reason for the lack of citizen participation through mechanisms such as public hearings that are not continuous processes. Because they take place on one occasion only, they will always prove inconvenient for some and rarely convenient for the old, the ill, and disabled.

The two other main responses were failure to attend because of lack of interest or belief that presence at the hearing would have no effect (some believed the meeting would be propaganda, others felt incapable of changing the

123

plan). This response indicates once again the assessment of lack of power to affect official action.

The residents' assessment of the influence of neighborhood organizations on official action is tabulated in Table 4.5. Over one-third believed that neighborhood organizations could not change an urban renewal plan opposed by the majority of the community. Of these, almost two-thirds held that community organizations were themselves to blame for their lack of effectiveness (because of their lack of unity and power). The remaining third held the government responsible for being unresponsive to the demands of the organizations. Thus failure to participate could, in large part, be explained by the feeling that participation is futile.

Table 4.5 Efficacy of Neighborhood Organizations to Change an Urban Renewal Plan

Response	Percentage (N=103)
Effective	54%
Not effective	35
Don't know	11
Total	100%

SUMMARY

The last three chapters have looked to the limits of individually initiated access to bureaucracy. We have discovered that the intended beneficiaries of a law are frequently faced with obstacles to its initiation. The obstacles, greater for the poor and uneducated, vary with the situation.

In this chapter we turned to the urban renewal situation, which, through the requirement of citizen participation, seemed at first to shift the burden of initiating access from the individual to bureaucracy. However, in Madison Park over one-half of the residents interviewed were ignorant of the urban renewal plan and how to participate in its formulation.

The urban renewal experience, therefore, instead of illustrating how obstacles might be overcome, served to emphasize the limits of citizen access to bureaucracy and the relatively greater limits that confront the urban poor, particularly the poorly educated. Many citizens possessed a limited willingness or capacity to involve themselves in community affairs and organizations. More than three out of four residents had never participated in any neighborhood organization. The lack of involvement extended to communication with government officials.

The reason for this low degree of participation might in part be the BRA's perfunctory attitude toward the requirement of citizen participation. Madison Park might also not be a particularly representative community. However, the characteristics revealed are confirmed by other reports, and by attitudes encountered in our earlier discussions: feelings of inability to influence government policy, and limited resources that allow formal participation.

What conclusions can we draw from this information about limited access? We have considered that "full" participation may not be possible or desirable. In welfare, for example, excessive claiming of rights and benefits might "destroy the system as effectively as armed rebellion."[104] It is important to know, however, that "rights" granted in law may not in practice be utilized. Armed with this knowledge, and with information about the specific factors that deter a greater level of participation, we may be able to assess whether obstacles impede the intended beneficiaries (or any class of beneficiaries) from receiving the benefits, whether such impediments are fairly placed, whether the obstacles might also impede other purposes, and what techniques may be employed to reduce the obstacles. These matters will be discussed in later chapters.

Notes

1. 68 Stat. 623, 42 U.S.C. § 145(1)(a) (1958).
2. 63 Stat. 413, 43 U.S.C. § 1441 (1958).
3. *Ibid.*, § 2. See S. Greer, *Urban Renewal and American Cities* (1965); and L. Friedman, *Government and Slum Housing* (1967).
4. *Ibid.*, § 3.
5. Apparently due to the exodus of the relatively wealthy city-dwellers to the suburbs and the simultaneous influx of lower-class mainly black residents. Greer, *op. cit.*, chap. 1. For the legislative history of the 1949 act, see A. Foard and H. Fefferman, "Federal Urban Renewal Legislation," 25 *Law and Contemp. Probs.* 635 (1960). See also, "Citizen Participation in Urban Renewal," 66 *Colum. L. Rev.* 485, 489 (1966).
6. 68 Stat. 627 (1954), 42 U.S.C. §§ 1453(a), 1460(e), (f) (Supp. V, 1958). See W. Sogg and W. Wertheimer, "Legal and Governmental Issues in Urban Renewal," 72 *Harv. L. Rev.* 504 (1959).
7. Greer, *op. cit.*, at 6. The process involves acquisition by the LPA of land in a designated area, the demolition of structures on the land, and the subsequent conveyance of the land to a private entrepreneur bound to develop it in accordance with the plan.
8. 48 Stat. 201 (1934), as amended, 42 U.S.C. §§ 401-33 (1952), as amended, 42 U.S.C. §§ 1411d-35 (Supp. V, 1958).
9. 50 Stat. 888 (1937), 42 U.S.C. § 1441 (1958).
10. 68 Stat. 623, 42 U.S.C. § 145 (1)(a) (1958).
11. *Ibid.*, at (1)(c). HHFA *Urban Renewal Manual*, c. 43, p. 1. Another innovation introduced by the 1954 Act was the allocation of 10% of the grants-in-aid for nonresidential purposes. The 1961 amendments increased this figure to 30% and made provision for a comprehensive renewal plan to encompass the entire city. 63 Stat. 413, 42 U.S.C. § 1441 (1958). The requirements for a "workable program" are (1) codes and ordinances; (2) comprehensive community plan; (3) neighborhood analysis; (4) administrative organization; (5) financing; (6) relocation planning; and (7) citizen participation. See C. Rhyne, "The Workable Program: A Call for Community Improvement," 25 *Law and Contemp. Probs.* 685, 690-691 (1960). For a critique of urban renewal by a conservative economist, see M. Anderson, *The Federal Bulldozer* (1964). For a more balanced critique, see H. Gans, "The Failure of Urban Renewal," *Commentary* vol. 39, no. 4, p. 4 (1965).
12. *Mass. Gen. Laws*, c. 121 § 2600 (1957). See L. Keyes, *The Rehabilitation Planning Game* (1969), which describes three urban renewal projects undertaken in Boston's South End, Charlestown, and Washington Park.
13. *Mass. Stats.*, c. 1950s I (1957), as amended, St. 1960, c. 652 §§ 12-14. *Mass. Gen. Laws* c. 121A (1966 Supp.). The BRA then consisted of five unpaid members—four appointed by the mayor and one by the State Housing Board.

Officially Initiated Access

14. Boston City Planning Board, *Preliminary Report—1950: General Plan for Boston*, (1950).

15. "Boston," 120 (6) *Architectural Forum*, 66 (1964).

16. Keyes, *op. cit.*, at 26.

17. Gans, *op. cit.*

18. For an account of the election in which Collins defeated Powers see M. Levin, *The Alienated Voter: Politics in Boston*, (1962). See also M. Meyerson and E. Banfield, *Boston: The Job Ahead*, (1966).

19. For a fuller account of Logue's background, appointment in Boston, and strategies, see Keyes, *op. cit.* See also, W. McQuade, "Urban Renewal in Boston," in J. Q. Wilson, ed., *Urban Renewal, the Record and the Controversy*, at 259 (1966); Wilson, "Planning and Politics, Citizen Participation in Urban Renewal," *op. cit.*, at 407.

20. Keyes, *op. cit.* at 29.

21. Wilson, *op. cit.*

22. *Mass. Ann. Laws*, c. 212 § § 26KK (Supp. 1966).

23. *Ibid.*, §26ZZ. With findings that (1) federal aid is necessary, (2) the plan provides maximum opportunity for the participation of private enterprise, (3) the plan conforms to a general plan for the community, and (4) the plan provides for adequate parks and recreation facilities. 42 U.S.C. § 1455(a) (Supp. IV, 1962).

24. *Ibid.* See U.S.C. Title 5, c. IIa-I, § 624 a-b (1964 Supp.).

25. See H. Osgood and A. Zwerner, "Rehabilitation and Conservation." 25 *Law and Contemp. Probs.* 711 (1960). In June 1968, however, the Second Circuit allowed several persons to bring a class action challenging allegedly inadequate relocation of persons to be displaced by an urban renewal project. Norwalk CORE v. Norwalk Redevelopment Agency, 395F. 2d 920 (2d Cir. 1968). See "Family Relocation in Urban Renewal," 82 *Harv. L. Rev.* 864 (1969); "Judicial Review of Displacee Relocation in Urban Renewal," 77 *Yale L.J.* 966 (1968).

26. C. 121A *Mass. Gen. Laws* (1966 Supp.). In Electronics Corp. of America v. City Council of Cambridge, 204 N.E. 2d 707, 348 Mass. 583 (1965), it was held that a business concern had no standing to object to a project when the BRA was "merely studying the area and had not made application for state approval."

27. 348 U.S. 26, 32 (1954).

28. 332 Mass. 259, 124 N.E. 2d 528 (1955).

29. Moskow v. Boston Redevelopment Authority, 349 Mass. 1213, 210 N.E. 2d 699, *cert. denied* 282 U.S. 983 (1965).

30. See K. C. Davis, "The Requirements of a Trial-Type Hearing," 70 *Harv. L. Rev.* 193 (1956-1957); Note, *Yale L. J.* 1080 (1964).

31. Moskow v. Boston Redevelopment Authority, *op. cit.*

32. *Ibid.*, note 11.

33. The LPA's plan could in theory be invalidated if citizen participation were found to be absent. At the time of this study, however, federal officials seemed reluctant to overthrow a plan which

127

had been endorsed by the Boston City Council on the ground of lack of citizen participation. The New York Regional Office of HUD bowed to the expertise of the city council, which "represents the will of the people of the city," to determine the existence of citizen participation. Interview with Area Coordinator, Boston Area, New York Regional Office, Department of Housing and Urban Development. The guidelines under the later *HUD Handbook Workable Program for Community Improvement*, RHA 7100.1 (October 1968) are more specific and might be more strictly enforced.

34. This approach was implicit in the report to President Eisenhower that resulted in the 1954 Workable Program and urged that "We should not try to pattern all urban residential areas on the stereotype of the neat, middle-class residential suburb, geared to the values and status-aspirations of its inhabitants and centered about children." President's Advisory Committee on Governmental Housing Policies and Programs, "Recommendations," at 132 (1953).

35. See F. Piven, "Participation of Residents in Neighborhood Community-Action Programs," in H. Spiegel, ed., *Citizen Participation in Urban Development*, at 113 (1968).

36. R. Dahl, *Who Governs*, at 131 (1961). "They're muscular because they control wealth, they're muscular because they control industries, represent banks . . . head up labor . . . represent the intellectual portions of the community."

37. *Ibid.*, at 131-132.

38. *Ibid.*, at 131.

39. *Ibid.*, at 133. *Cf.* P. Rossi and R. Dentler, *The Politics of Urban Renewal* (1959), who state that the participation of citizens "provides an important element of mass commitment to a plan, which aids in providing support for the notion of a general public interest overriding individual interest and in preventing the formation of dissident local groups." (at 287).

40. Economic Opportunity Act of 1964, 78 Stat. 516, 45 U.S.C. § § 113(a)(b) (1964).

41. See, e.g., D. Moynihan, *Maximum Feasible Misunderstanding* (1969); A. Yarmolinsky, "The Beginnings of OEO," in J. Sundquist, ed., *On Fighting Poverty*, at 34 (1969); J. Sundquist, "Origins of the War on Poverty," *ibid.*, at 6.

42. See M. Rein and S. Miller, "Citizen Participation and Poverty," 1 *Connecticut L. Rev.* 221 (1968).

43. E. Cahn and J. Cahn, "Citizen Participation," in H. Spiegel, ed., *Citizen Participation in Urban Development*, 211 at 219 (1968).

44. Robert Lane [*Political Life* (1958)] states that it has been found that extremist politics such as communism in the United States helped a person to legitimize and rationalize his aggression. According to Lane, "Just as political therapy is possible in extreme political situations, it is also possible for those who need the 'satisfaction of performing civic duties' " (at 339). It might be noted that the recent HUD regulations RHA 7100.1, *op. cit.*, note 306, consider it "essential

that the participation be satisfying, rewarding, and not frustrating" c. 7, p. 1. Compare the remarks of Erich Fromm: "The worker can become an active, interested and responsible participant only if he can have influence on the decisions which bear upon his individual work situation and the whole enterprise. His alienation from work can be overcome only if ... he is not the object of a command, but if he becomes a responsible *subject who employs capital.* The principal point here is not *ownership of the means of production* but *participation in management and decision making.* E. Fromm, *The Sane Society*, at 281 (1955). (Emphasis in original.)

45. E.g., in the most recent HUD *Handbook, op. cit.*

46. Reference is being made here to the individuals with whom the BRA will participate *directly*. In theory all the citizens of an area or of the city will be represented by the "representative" committees, and will thus participate indirectly. In order to understand the mechanics of the process, however, it is necessary to identify those with whom direct contact will be made by the local public agency.

47. See. M. Edelman, *The Symbolic Uses of Politics* (1964), and M. Lipsky, "Protest as a Political Resource," 62(4) *Amer. J. Polit. Sci.* 1144 (1968).

48. Compare Sherry Arnstein's concept of a "ladder" of citizen participation. Arnstein's categories differ from those described here in that they fail to distinguish between the purposes of citizen participation, the potential citizen groups involved, and the mechanisms of participation. S. Arnstein, "A Ladder of Citizen Participation," A.I.P.J., 216 (July 1969).

49. Department of Housing and Urban Development, *Workable Program for Community Improvement*, at 1 (1966).

50. *Ibid.*

51. "[The citizens] should be able to communicate the interests of their group ... to the committee ... and should also be capable of explaining to their group or organization the policies and programs put forward by official bodies. ..." *Ibid.*

52. *HUD Handbook*, "Workable Program for Community Improvement," RHA 7100.1, c. 7, p. 1 (October 1968).

53. *Ibid.*, at 2.

54. See Demonstration Cities and Metropolitan Development Act, P.L. 89-754, 80 Stat. 1255 ss. 103 (a)(2) (1966). For an account of the latest citizen participation requirements under this act, see Department of Housing and Urban Development, Model Cities Administration, Technical Assistance Bulletin, No. 3 (December 1968).

55. *Ibid.*

56. The following account is drawn from interviews conducted in November 1966 with various members of the staff of the BRA, including the project director of the Madison Park project, and various members of Urban Planning Aid, Inc. The account is also based upon an article by Melvin B. Miller in the *Bay State Banner*, Saturday, December 3, 1966, p. 1, col. 3; p. 2, col. 1-3; and BRA, "Summary Report on the

Proposed Campus High School" (July 1966). The interviews referred to were conducted during February and March 1968 with a random sample of 103 adult members of Madison Park households who had been living in the area from the start of the urban renewal project activity in mid-1966.

57. BRA, "Diagnostic Report, Residents of the Proposed Campus High School" (October 1966).

58. This statistic and those following are deduced from the interview sample referred to in note 56.

59. See generally, Metropolitan Area Planning Council, The Commonwealth of Massachusetts, *Social Structures and Human Problems in the Boston Metropolitan Area* (1965).

60. Seventy percent of the whites interviewed were over 50 years of age, compared with only 38.3 percent of the blacks.

61. For an account of this procedure see W. Sogg and W. Wertheimer, "Legal and Governmental Issues in Urban Renewal," 72 *Harv. L. Rev.* 504, 519-23 (1959).

62. Interview with Madison Park area project director.

63. *Bay State Banner*, Saturday, December 3, 1966, p. 1, col. 7-8.

64. Urban Planning Aid, "Statement of Purpose" (June 1966).

65. The following account of the public hearing is based largely upon BRA, "Stenographic Record, Campus High School in Madison Park Urban Renewal Area, Before the Boston Redevelopment Authority," July 25, 1966.

66. See the testimony of Ralph Smith, Shirley Spolinsky, and Hazel McArthy, "Stenographic Record," *op. cit.*, pp. 43-51.

67. Memorandum to Boston Redevelopment Authority from Edward J. Logue, Development Administrator, September 15, 1966.

68. *Mass. Acts of 1966*, § § 1-14.

69. Logue memorandum, *op. cit.*

70. Memorandum to Boston Redevelopment Authority from Edward J. Logue, Development Administrator, October 11, 1966.

71. The following account of statements made at the hearing relies both upon personal observation of the sessions of the hearing and upon BRA, Stenographic Record, Madison Campus High School, Before the Committee on Urban Renewal, November 16, 1966.

72. Stenographic Record, *op. cit.*, at 22-31.

73. *Ibid.*, at 107.

74. *Ibid.*, at 108-109. A BRA survey, however, discovered that 51 percent of the nonwhite households, but only 24 percent of the white households, wished to remain in the area. "Diagnostic Report," *op. cit.*, at 28-29. My own survey more closely supports Fellman's findings, showing that 63 percent of the total sample would prefer to remain in the area, with 37 percent preferring to move. Seventy-two percent of the black and 47 percent of the white sample wished to stay. But these attitudes were expressed 18 months after the BRA and Urban Planning Aid, Inc., surveys, and after a large exodus from the area.

75. Fellman was supported by Robert Goodman, Assistant Professor in Urban Planning and Architecture at the Massachusetts Institute of Technology, Stenographic Record, *op. cit.*, at 116.

76. Boston *Globe*, Thursday, November 17, 1966, p. 7, col. 1.

77. Boston *Herald*, Friday, November 18, 1966, p. 3, col. 1. UPA is based in Cambridge, across the Charles River from Boston.

78. *Ibid.* This statement is partially explained (by UPA members) as being due to Logue's mistaken belief that the UPA activity was a class exercise for Goodman's planning students who were sitting in on the hearing.

79. Boston *Globe*, Thursday, November 24, 1966, p. 35, cols. 1-8.

80. Boston *Globe*, Wednesday, November 30, 1966, p. 2, col. 8.

81. Boston *Herald*, Friday, December 2, 1966, p. 17, cols. 1-2.

82. This was done contrary to the advice of the advocate planners. In fact, the LRCC excluded UPA from their meeting with the BRA.

83. *Bay State Banner*, Saturday, January 14, 1967, p. 6, cols. 5-8.

84. This concept will be discussed below. See Edelman, *op. cit.*, and Lipsky, *op. cit.*

85. "Lecture Review: Mr. Stainton Discusses Urban Renewal," "Connection," p. 18 (December 18, 1963).

86. Forty-two of the 85. Eight residents spoke at the meeting.

87. Wilson, *op. cit.*, at 417.

88. For example, Scott Greer concludes that there is a "lack of broadly based support for urban renewal, or even an understanding of the program," *op. cit.*, at 40.

89. Interviews.

90. H. Zorbaugh, *The Gold Coast and the Slum*, at 198 (1928), cf. M. Follet, *The New State* (1918).

91. Zorbaugh, *op. cit.*

92. M. White, in *Street Corner Society: The Social Structure of an Italian Slum* (1943), and H. Gans, *Urban Villagers* (1962). See generally, M. Axelrod, "Urban Structure and Social Participation," in P. Hatt and A. Reiss, eds., *Cities and Society*, at 722 (1964). For a recent work, see G. Suttles, *The Social Order of the Slum* (1968). See generally, C. Valentine, *Culture and Poverty* (1968).

93. Stenographic Record, South End Urban Renewal Plan, Before Boston Redevelopment Authority, *op. cit.*, at 161-164.

94. In response to the question: "How much interest would you say that you take in what goes on here in this neighborhood? For example, in changes, in improvement, or in neighborhood problems?" Thirty-eight % were very interested, 26% fairly interested, 22% not too interested, and 14% not interested at all.

95. Twenty-nine of 37 with less than eight years' schooling.

96. Eighteen of 35 with a high school education.

97. Two of 37.

98. Fourteen of 35.

99. For example, 16 of 37 (43%) of those with less than eight

years' education, and 10 of 35 (29%) of those with a high school education socialized with their neighbors once or twice a year or less frequently.

100. See generally A. Almond and S. Verba, *The Civic Culture*, chap. 7 (1963), and L. Milbrath, *Political Participation*, at 70-80 (1965).

101. E. Banfield, *The Unheavenly City* (1970).

102. Eighty-two percent of the sample agreed with the statement, "Sometimes politics and government seem so complicated that a person like me can't understand what's going on." The project director of the BRA's South End urban renewal project stated that participation there from a group of poor Puerto Ricans was virtually nil, "probably because they have enough problems of their own to worry about."

103. They are thus, in Banfield's scheme, "situationally" rather than "cognitively" present-oriented. For a study of the kinds of incentives necessary to maintain participation in organization, see M. Olson, *The Logic of Collective Action* (1965). See also J. Q. Wilson and P. Clark, "Incentive Systems: A Theory of Organizations," 6 *Admin. Sci. Q.* 129 (1961).

104. L. Friedman. "Social Welfare Legislation: An Introduction," 21 *Stan. L. Rev.* 217, 234-235 (1969).

5

The Functional Limits of Legality

Until now we have been discussing the strategic merits and demerits of rules and adjudication as devices to control administrative discretion. The last three chapters have examined, in the light of concrete situations, the specific question of access to law and bureaucracy. The argument about rules and adjudication cannot be settled, however, on the basis of a simple balancing between probable costs and benefits. Whatever their abstract merits in achieving standards of justice, fairness, or convenience, rules and adjudication might simply be inappropriate techniques for decision about certain problems. In other words, we might hypothesize that there are certain problems inherently unsuited to decision by rule and adjudication. This chapter will explore this hypothesis, looking to the decision about "need" in welfare for concrete illustration, and presenting a model that illustrates administrative decision making in the light of our findings.

We have seen that the "legalized" decision involves governance by rule. Adjudication involves decision by reference either to a rule, standard, or principle. The hypothesis raised now is that these decision-making guides (principles, rules, and standards) are not appropriate for solving certain kinds of problems. It should be repeated, however, that the propositions advanced here constitute "ideal-typical" characterizations. Decisions may be made in an adjudicative setting without the elements of participation or reference to rule, principle, or standard that Fuller requires. It is suggested, however, that the integrity of the process of adjudication will be eroded or destroyed if the reality often veers too far from the ideal.

PRINCIPLES

Principles arise mainly in the context of judicial decision making.[1] They involve normative moral standards by which rules can be evaluated and are frequently expressed in maxims such as "No man shall profit by his own wrong," or "He who comes to court shall come with clean hands." They have developed in the judicial context over time and are less suited to administrative decision because they do not address economic, social, or political criteria, but rather justice and fairness in the judicial situation. A principle that may arise in the administrative context would be the maxim "Like cases shall receive like treatment."

RULES

Roscoe Pound defined a rule as a "legal precept attaching a definite detailed legal consequence to a definite detailed state of fact."[2] We have seen that the process of legalization involves the transformation of broad policies into rules. Policies are statements of general objectives, such as "to provide decent, safe and sanitary housing," or "to prevent unsafe driving." The policy is legalized as the various elements of housing and driving are specified, providing, for example, for hot and cold running water, 70 degree heat, maximum speed limits, and one-way streets. A rule is thus a concrete general direction in which legal consequences are appended to the happening or nonhappening of an event or the occurrence of a situation.[3] The enforcement of a rule (such as the maximum speed rule) requires the event or situation (the driver's speed) to be determined factually.

Although rules are concrete guides for decision addressing themselves to specific fact-situations, their application cannot always be mechanical. As we have seen, a parking meter may simply register the end of a time limit. But because rules are purposive devices (they are techniques to effectuate a broader policy) and because language is largely uncertain in its application to situations that cannot be foreseen, the applier of a rule will frequently have a degree of discretion in interpreting its scope.[4] In doing so, he will go beyond the wording of the rule in order to discover and weigh controlling principles and policies. He will not be passive but will himself be an agent in the rule's elaboration.[5]

What are the limits of rule-governed conduct? The essential limit arises as a corollary of the fact that a rule is a general direction, applicable to a number of "like" situations that may arise in the future. Although rules may contain exceptions, they are not tailored primarily to individual circumstances; they view the individual to whom the rule applies as one of a class or category. The speed rule does not distinguish between a person exceeding the speed limit in the rush hour and the person doing so in the early hours of the morning. According to the letter of the rule, the speeder is a violater in both cases.

The corollary, therefore, of the impersonal nature of rules is that they are unsuited to the guidance of situations where the activity is nonrecurring or unique. Where a rule is to be applied "without regard to persons" (in Weber's phrase), it is unsuited to personalized, individual application. Personalized application means unique, non recurring handling, because so many variables are to be taken into account that practically speaking no two cases are the same.

For example, university seats could be filled according to a rule specifing admission on the basis of past grades. This would allow a disinterested, objective, admission procedure. However, if qualities such as personality, leadership potential, or potential for future development were required, it would be much harder to frame rules that specify these qualities in advance. Similarly, where a decision is required that takes into account the "whole man"[6] in order to determine suitability for political leadership or to provide specific rehabilitative care, or where a remedy is required that can be applied against the background of a person's history and life-situation,[7] then an impersonal rule prescribing certain objective "impersonal" guides is not suitable. James Q. Wilson has described the impossibility of formulating rules to "guide" the police patrolman's discretion in a situation of order-maintenance. He points out that rules prescribing certain courses of action ("don't use a racial epithet," or "don't hit a man except in self-defense") are more useful in guiding conduct than rules that prescribe affirmative action. Nevertheless,

no very useful—certainly no complete—set of instructions can be devised as to what the officer *should* do with, say, quarrelling lovers. Defining a policy in such matters is difficult, not because the police have not given much thought to the matters or because they do not know how they should be handled, but because so much depends on the particular circumstances of time, place, event, and personality. Psychiatrists do not use "how to do it" manuals, and they have the advantage of dealing with people at leisure, over protracted periods of time, and in periods of relative calm.[8]

STANDARDS

Standards are directives more general than rules. Their purpose is to specify policies while retaining the benefit of flexibility. A *rule* will provide for a definite speed limit (say, 55 miles per hour). A *standard* will provide that drivers must exercise "due care." Application of a standard thus requires, in addition to the finding of a fact in a particular situation (how fast was the vehicle going?), a qualitative appraisal of the fact, in terms of its probable consequences or moral justification (does that speed in those circumstances imply lack of "due care"?).

Thus where a housing by-law, for example, contains rules specifying precise requirements, such as minimum winter heating and number of inside toilets, all that is necessary for its application is a determination of whether the house in question fulfills the rules. A standard requiring a house to be in a "fit state of habitation," however, requires both a factual determination and a qualitative appraisal—what was the condition of the house? Does that condition constitute a "fit" state of habitation? Standards may be rendered more precise by criteria, which are normally weighed against one another. For example, the housing by-laws may constitute one set of criteria for determining whether a particular house is "fit for habitation."

The distinguishing feature of standards is their flexibility and susceptibility to change over time. In 1955, for example, "average" and "prudent" university administrators probably had little difficulty in determining a standard for "neat" dress in university lecture halls. Obviously, skirts for women and collars and ties for men were essential criteria of neatness. Some years later, however, the standard changed, allowing trousers for ladies and open collars for men. Paul Freund, in his discussion of the elaboration of constitutional standards, refers to the

proud solace of the German artist who exclaimed "if nothing else at least I am contemporary!" Certainly it is not discreditable in a judge, even a judge interpreting the Constitution to be a contemporary. Vistas grow, perspectives lengthen, reflection deepens, and new meanings come to seem fitting for such projecting terms as "liberty" or "due process of law."[9]

What are the limits to the use of standards in making decisions? The first arises where it is not meaningful to refer to a general community consensus. In commercial law, for example, the requirements of "fairness" can be meaningfully elaborated by drawing on conceptions and evaluations shared by the community of traders.[10] However, a community consensus is often absent, or opinion may be in a state of transition. In such cases the decision maker, despite the legitimacy of his role as an agent in the articulation of standards, is likely to be justifiably criticized if he boldly declares a standard to exist. When behavior that was formerly clearly labelled either as desirable and right, or as undesirable and wrong, becomes transformed into a matter of preference and taste, a standard cannot be meaningfully articulated. Standards depend for their meaningful application upon the existence of a community norm. Thus it might be impossible today to specify the requirements of "immoral" sexual conduct—Does it include homosexual conduct between consenting adults?[11] Or pornography—Is certain literature of "social importance"? Or "neatness"—Will unruly hair qualify? Where a standard is expressed in terms that specifically incorporate a question of individual taste, the difficulty of applying it is thrown into high relief. Thus in one case a judge was not able to enforce a covenant restricting the erection of "any building of unseemly description."[12] Zoning for aesthetically pleasing architectural standards poses similar problems.

As we have seen in connection with the limits of rules, a situation to which a general direction may be applied must be capable of categorization in a class with "like" cases. Similarly, where standards are to be applied by comparing an instance in question with like instances, either those that are directly competing (as in a FM station license application) or those that exist in the community, one must be able to put instances to be compared in a similar class or category. Judges of an agricultural show, for example, would find it very hard to select in a meaningful way the best fruit or the best animal. Pears must be judged against pears, pigs against pigs. At a sporting event, high jumpers cannot easily be compared with long jumpers, though they have obvious affinities compared with long-distance runners. In a license application a meaningful comparative evaluation could scarcely be made between an applicant who would provide 24 hours of Bach and one who would provide news during that time (assuming an otherwise balanced spectrum). Similarly, the standard of "due care," while in general laying down an objective test of conduct,[13] will not allow a child to be judged by the same standards as an adult.[14]

As with rules, unique or nonrecurring situations are similarly unsuited to evaluation by reference to a standard. For example, it would not be difficult to assess the "fair rent" of a conventional house in a conventional neighborhood. If the house was unique, experimental, and with little market appeal, despite the fact that it was more expensive to build than the conventional houses around it, it would not be suited to comparison with them precisely because it was not "alike." The decision maker in such a case would probably decide the case by reference to the market value criterion, thus relying on the "invisible hand" of the free market to decide for us in a case unsuited to decision according to standard.[15] The same problem might be encountered by arbitrators attempting to set a "fair rate" for a unique job.[16] Judge Friendly has described some of the problems that lie in the search for guiding standards to control the allocative tasks of the Federal Communications Commission:

The job that congress gave the Commission was somewhat comparable to asking the Board of the Metropolitan Opera Association to decide, after public hearing and with a reasoned opinion, whether the public convenience, interest, or necessity would be served by having the prima donna role on the opening night sung by ... Tebaldi, Sutherland, or one of several winners of high American awards.[17]

In order to assess some of the limits to legal decision making in light of an example, the decision about need in the welfare process will now be considered.

THE LEGAL CONTROL OF THE WELFARE PROCESS

Charles Reich's call for welfare as "property" has received much attention.[18] He lists two main abuses of current welfare law: first, administrative behavior that is frequently unconstitutional or contrary to statutory terms; and second, interference with welfare recipients' interests, such as privacy and moral behavior, which have not been classified as legal rights. Since the appearance of Reich's articles some of the abuses he specifies have been challenged in the courts and remedied.[19] In order to secure his suggested "property rights" in welfare on a continuing basis, however, Reich and his supporters propose that (1) eligibility criteria be decided in advance rather than on a case-by-case basis and (2) "full adjudicatory procedures" be utilized to protect individual "rights."[20]

We have considered some of the merits of rules and adjudication. Some of these are claimed for welfare "rights." Advocates would remove the determination for or against a grant from the discretionary ambit of a caseworker. The claimant would then no longer be a suppliant recipient of a privilege, dependent upon its beneficent exercise by the caseworker, but the claimant of a "right" or "entitlement." If the rules were federally determined, regional disparities would disappear; like cases would be treated alike. We could then claim that because all were entitled to a predetermined measure of need (whether provided through the present welfare system or by means of a guaranteed income), poverty had been eliminated from our society.

The corresponding defects of rules and adjudication have already been discussed. The functional possibility of solving major welfare problems by submitting decisions concerning needs to predetermined rules or adjudication will now be considered.

Rule-Determined Need

When we attribute a "need" to a person, we indicate the lack of something it would be detrimental not to supply to that person.[21] "X needs sleep" implies that lack of sleep would be injurious to X. The term "need" normally implies that the lack of something prevents the person from maintaining a community norm. To say that X "needs" food is to say that he will not measure up to a community standard unless he gets it. To say that X "wants" food is simply to describe his state of mind or his claim for a perceived or felt desire. Wants are therefore individually perceived or felt needs, which may or may not correspond with community-determined needs.

Any law providing for the disbursement of scarce resources must obviously set a cutoff point for eligibility and for those wants that may be satisfied by the resources allocated. Laws providing for income maintenance would establish rules that set up the qualifications for assistance, the age of sixty-five, for example, for eligibility for Old Age Assistance. In addition, rules would have to be made that set limits to the amount of aid to be granted and the technique of determining the amount. We have seen that in Massachusetts, at the time of this study, the rules set a list of "basic budgetary needs" that would be provided to a welfare recipient.[22] In addition to this predetermined list of needs to satisfy persons possessing a given set of personal and financial characteristics, the rules also allow for a residual category of "special need" to be determined upon request on a "casework basis" at the discretion of the caseworker.[23]

In Massachusetts the provision of "basic budgetary need" constitutes an attempt to predetermine a catalogue of wants that welfare will satisfy. In drafting this catalogue a political choice has been made as to which of a number of different categories of wants are to be satisfied.

It is neither accurate nor realistic, in a technologically developed state, to consider need merely in terms of the basic physical necessities. The psychologist Maslow, for example, has posited a simple hierarchy of needs. First to be satisfied are (1) the physical needs, such as food and shelter. Then two other "lower" needs arise, namely, (2) safety needs and (3) affection or belongingness needs. After these the "higher needs" demand to be satisfied. These are (4) self-esteem needs and (5) self-actualization or self-development needs.[24] Maslow stresses the fact that even though "lower" needs are satisfied, the satisfaction of "higher" needs does not become any less urgent. In fact, they become more urgent, because the person is no longer concerned with "lower" needs.

As to what degree the hierarchy of needs should be satisfied by public assistance, the Massachusetts welfare system has responded by providing financial assistance to satisfy basic physical needs according to its own calculation of these needs. The satisfaction of other needs will be assisted by the "social service" schemes, or not at all.

The next question is which of the basic physical or psychological needs to satisfy. Some wants, for example, may be artifically stimulated or created through "relative deprivation"[25] and may not be intrinsic to man's physical nature. In *The Affluent Society*, John Kenneth Galbraith[26] challenges the conventional wisdom of our time, which contended that the urgency of wants does not diminish appreciably as more of them are satisfied. Galbraith is critical of the fact that the concept of satiation has little place in economics and turned his own argument upon the "dependence effect."[27] This concept asserts that a great part of the wants still unsatisfied in modern society are not wants that are experienced spontaneously by the individual but rather are wants created by the very process by which they are satisfied. The consumer is subject to the forces of advertising and emulation by which production creates its own demand. Keynes is cited in support through his statement that the needs of human beings "fall into two classes—those needs which are absolute in the sense that we feel them whatever the situation of our fellow human beings may be, and those which are relative only in that their satisfaction lifts us above, makes us feel superior to, our fellows."[28]

To take Galbraith's dependence effect as given in our society and even to admit the truth of his proposition that "one man's consumption is another man's wish,"[29] does not help us in deciding which of a person's wants should be satisfied before others of that same individual or other individuals are satisfied. In other words even if we concede that some wants are "artificially" stimulated and that others arise from "relative deprivation," we are still not able to separate the "real" from the "artificial." And as long as the "artificial" exists, it may be a more intense want to the consumer than the "real."[30]

For example, a person's desire for an electric razor, "artificially" stimulated by clever television advertising, might prove more intense than his desire for a winter coat. The welfare department's decision to list a winter coat as an allowed need but not an electric razor is based on the department's assessment of an allowable and legitimate need. In this example, however, the more intense of the two wants would be unfulfilled.

Economists examining a person's preferences would employ the "utility function" to assess the change in a person's marginal satisfaction that results from the acquisition of a commodity. However, this marginal utility may depend upon the individual's consumption of other commodities. For example, to a person who hasn't eaten for two days, the marginal utility of a slice of bread would be high; whereas to a person who has just completed a hearty breakfast, the marginal utility of the slice would be small.

A rule providing that a television set is not a "need" would, according to utility theory, have the effect of assigning to a television set a utility value below that of "need." However, because individual need, like marginal utility, is calculated in terms of preferences, priorities, and marginal satisfaction, it cannot be determined accurately either by a lump-sum figure based on a predetermined value or by a catalogue of items that either will or will not be deemed to constitute need.

For example, the marginal utility of a television set cannot be ascertained in isolation. The intensity of a person's desire for a television set might be affected by whether he already owns a radio; in the same way a person's preference for a steak for lunch may be affected by the size of his breakfast. A mother who has no other source of reasonably well spoken English or of education in the home might place a much higher value upon the television set than would a person who wanted the set simply to watch late-night entertainment shows. A mother who wanted the set to help keep her children off the streets at night might place a higher value on it than would a person who wanted it because the Joneses next door have one.

These examples illustrate why rules are inadequate to determine individually perceived or felt needs. We have seen that rules necessitate application to "like" categories or classes. Except for the basic biological and physical needs, individual needs are not suited to categorization. They depend upon personal preferences, priorities, and marginal satisfactions. Mrs. X's desire for a television set for her children's education might in fact be more intense than her desire for certain basic foods or clothing for herself. For welfare officials to say that a television set is *not* a need and a winter coat every three years *is* a need is to assign an objective value to something that can only be measured by individual and subjective considerations and that therefore is unsuited to predetermination by rule.[31]

If we are concerned with providing *any* list of predetermined needs, simply to reduce caseworker discretion and to obtain any other advantages inherent in rules *qua* rules, then the intensity of individual desires will not concern us. This is, however, not the position of the advocates of welfare "rights." They focus on the content of rights provided and expect that a basic minimum of individual preference ought to be fulfilled. Their aim is surely commendable. The possibility of achieving it is, however, slim. The Massachusetts experience demonstrates this fact.

Rule-Determined Need in Massachusetts

The Massachusetts "basic budgetary need" list includes food, rent, fuel and utilities, household supplies, clothing, personal care, and life insurance. Over and above the weekly payment which is supposed to cover these items, the caseworker had, during the period of this study, the discretion to provide for a client's "special need" (in practice, items such as household goods, a special diet, or emergency costs). During the summer of 1968, however, welfare rights groups, in a series of sit-ins at the district office, demanded guidelines of items they were entitled to claim.[32] As a result, statutory furniture and household guidelines were prepared. Forty-two items were listed with price limits.[33]

Because it is not possible to prepare an exhaustive catalogue of items, any attempt to do so would exclude many that might be, were they measurable, of greater value to the individual than those listed as allowable. For example, vacuum cleaners were not allowable in the Massachusetts regulations. One recipient, however, requested a vacuum cleaner for the purpose of eliminating the dust that caused her daughter's asthma. She was willing to forego a new (and needed) winter coat—an allowable item—in favor of the vacuum cleaner, which was not listed.

The result of rule-determined need was often thus to subvert the stated purposes of the program.[34] A recipient's son in one case, for example, had mild cerebral palsy. Her enterprising caseworker eventually found a school for retarded children that would aid greatly in the boy's rehabilitation. It was necessary for the mother to obtain a grant for school fees and carfare because the school was some distance from the recipient's home. The regulations make provision for granting school fees,[35] which the recipient was allowed, but make no mention of carfare, which was denied. The recipient attempted for a long time to gain admission for her son to the school and had obtained funds to send him there; yet she was thwarted because the rules made no mention of carfare.

Some limit to the needs that public assistance may fill must be established. But the capacity of rules to establish a catalogue of items (as was done in Massachusetts) providing for people's most intense wants is limited. Three reasons combine to cause this fact: First, as the above examples show, wants are highly individualistic. A vacuum cleaner, carfare, or a television set might be an intense want for Mrs. X but receive a low priority on Mrs. Y's preference scale. Second, wants are such that they are likely to be satisfied in the order of their immediacy and intensity. Third, welfare recipients are operating on the border between subsistence and starvation.

Together these three factors cause a situation that is typically and frequently faced by welfare officials: A recipient will be inclined to use any available funds for what is perceived as an immediate and urgent need, such as a new winter coat or summer camp for her child, even if the item was not authorized by the rules. A week later, however, the recipient might have no money to pay her rent. Rent is an allowable extra (being listed as a "basic budgetary need"), and the caseworker would be permitted to pay it, thus indirectly subsidizing the winter coat. The amount of the rent would then be subtracted from the recipient's budget for the next month, leaving her short of money to pay for other immediate needs and farther from the program's stated goal of independence and self-support.

Welfare recipients have no cushion of resources to fall back on. If they see fit to satisfy what they consider to be immediate and urgent needs at the expense of needs officially listed as legitimate, the department might be faced with the alternative of subsidizing the recipient's need or allowing her to starve. Caseworkers faced with this dilemma—and they constantly are—are forced to manipulate the system on their client's behalf.[36] Joseph Lyford, an observer of the welfare process on the west side of New York for many years, has said that caseworkers freely admit that they forge signatures and falsify reports so that they can circumvent red tape and give their clients needed help. "It is part of the conspiracy to get things done. The system cannot work without cheating."[37] The present study has revealed no incident of forgery or falsity by caseworkers. It has discovered, however, that caseworkers sympathetic to their clients would, for the reasons canvassed above, be inclined to find many of the rules about need obstructive.

In November 1968, a few months after the present case study was completed, the Massachusetts legislature's Committee on Social Welfare released a report on the state welfare system. The report listed "flagrant abuses" of the system.[38] One of the most flagrant was the fact that the Welfare Department paid overdue utility bills and back rent and issued extra food orders to recipients who ran out of money. The report claimed that recipients had "deliberately mismanaged" their budget, with the result that the Department of Welfare was paying rent and utility money twice.[39]

Just as it cannot be asserted with assurance that the caseworkers observed were not fraudulent, it cannot be asserted that the recipients observed were all totally honest. Except in a few marginal cases, however, no evidence of such behavior was discovered. It is not surprising, nevertheless, that apparent abuses of the welfare system are revealed. They arise less from any personal bad faith on the part of caseworkers or recipients than from the inherent incapacity of predetermined need to take into account the intensity of individual preferences.

The Adjudication of Need

We have seen that the caseworkers in Massachusetts had

147

discretion to determine a recipient's "special need." Four out of five cases were appealed on this issue. Although the opportunity to challenge a decision in an adjudicatory situation might contain merit, it also, as we have seen, contains defects. Neither of these points will be considered now. What will be considered is the suitability of adjudication to decide individual need.

Need is a standard. In order to assess whether a person is in need, the adjudicator will have to make both a factual determination (does the person lack the item in question?) and a qualitative evaluation (does the lack of the item constitute "need"?). Few special problems arise from the first of these determinations—proofs and arguments can easily be directed to the factual issue. For example, the issue of whether a person claiming special moving or travel expenses really did incur those expenses suits itself to a judicial determination.

It is in the qualitative evaluation of "need" that proofs and arguments cannot be meaningfully presented, at least if the claim is for more than basic physical need, where an objective standard in society might be assumed. Over and above these, however, individual desires are so unique that no objective standard can be found. Examples drawn from the cases demonstrate the unique character of welfare claims.

Mrs. A requested money to pay for her daughter's graduation expenses and repairs to her washing machine (both items were refused by the caseworker, reversed on appeal); Mrs. M requested money to pay for legal expenses in connection with her divorce suit (grant refused); Mrs. Q asked welfare to pay for a scalp treatment recommended by her doctor (grant refused); Mrs. S requested bunk beds in her children's room on the ground that it would provide more space in a crowded room (grant refused because the bed would accumulate dust, despite the fact that Mrs. S was described by the caseworker as "capable and efficient").

Evaluation of these claims as needs would have to be based upon the caseworker's or referee's assessment of the appellant's desires. No one but the claimant, however, is likely to be in a position to validate the intensity of the desire, which, as we have seen, depends on the marginal utility of the item to the appellant.[40] It may be that Mrs. X's desire for a television set to keep up with the Joneses is more intense than her desire for a winter coat. The intensity of her desire for a television set will also depend upon other subjective and personal factors, such as whether she already owns a radio. One caseworker was unwilling to concede the subjective nature of individual wants. Her client was requesting bookcases as a special need and had stated that her own and her children's books were cluttering their small apartment. The caseworker wrote in the case summary that her "adamant" client "obviously believes . . . that she is the best judge of what her needs are."

An objective standard by which to evaluate a claimant's need may occasionally be found. For example, a certain minimum of food might according to objective nutritional evaluations be considered basic. However, at the time of this study these items were provided through the basic budgetary calculation. It is doubtful, however, whether a community consensus about need beyond the basic physical needs could be ascertained through the adjudicative process. As we have seen, one man's necessity might be another man's luxury. Even if common usage could be assumed (for example, of television sets), does it follow that the item commonly used is considered a necessity by its users? What degree of community intensity do we require to call an item a need? Need is as difficult to ascertain through judicial techniques as other standards such as "morality," "neatness," or "beauty."

An objective issue to which proofs and arguments could be directed in assessing need is that of the legitimate cost of the item claimed. For example, the Welfare Department might prohibit the granting of certain items such as taxi transportation or automobiles on the ground that they would simply be too extravagant, even if motor transportation were conceded to be the most urgent of a recipient's desires. At the time of this study the district office did lay down one criterion, namely, a maximum of $100 per request. Claims for special need of items such as television sets, dishwashing machines, private school fees, legal fees, and a deposit on a new home were all refused as extravagant, either because their cost exceeded the $100 limit or for reasons of policy. The existence of the individually felt need, however, could not in any of the cases be effectively questioned.

Proofs and arguments could in theory be directed to the issue of interpersonal utility, attempting to demonstrate need or its absence by comparison with similarly situated cases. For example, the need for a television set could be shown by comparing the need of the present recipient with that of another recipient who had been either granted or denied one. Some appellants attempted to invoke such comparisons in support of their claims. The Mothers for Adequate Welfare were cataloguing instances of claims that were granted for items such as winter coats, winter clothes for children, or summer camp for recipients' children. The MAWS, who represented appellants at hearings, frequently cited such instances to support their appellants' claims.

Aside from the political usefulness of these claims, however, the demonstration of need by reference to comparative cases cannot be successfully accomplished through adjudication in view of mechanical as well as conceptual difficulties. The mechanical difficulty has to do first with the fact that past cases are not available because each case is confidential. If past decisions were published, this obstacle might be reduced. But even then, the subtle differences between each case in a matter so inherently individual could scarcely be calculated. The referee who stated that he would not "be bound by what happened yesterday" was implicitly acknowledging that today's and yesterday's case about need are often as distinct as pumpkins and pears.[43] The intensity of Mrs. X's desire for a television set will depend, as we have seen, upon subjective and personal factors. As an economist has pointed out,

Neither economics, nor, as far as I know, social science in general can contrive a measure of satisfaction that would make one comfortable about asserting that Mr. A, with very aristocratic tastes and only two Picassos, does not feel more deprivation from want of a third than does Mr. B, who hasn't been able to buy shoes for the last three years.[42]

In summary, the issue joined here was not whether welfare should be subjected to rules and adjudicative procedures as a check upon official discretion. The costs and benefits of legalization and judicialization have been considered. The author's view is that the costs involved (e.g., the potential dangers of legalism and the threat involved in the adversary confrontation between caseworker and recipient) will be far outweighed by the benefits gained by subjecting welfare officials to scrutiny and challenge. In this way official action that is unconstitutional or contrary to statutory terms might be remedied. We must bear in mind again that there may be a variety of obstacles to the utilization of the opportunity to challenge official action. A "right" to welfare, therefore, does not necessarily mean that the opportunity to exercise the right will, in practice, be either possible or free of costs. Nor does the right *qua* right speak to the content of the right, such as the generosity of the grant or the expressed or implied conditions attached to its receipt.

The issue that was joined here was whether individual need can be determined by rules or adjudication. Clearly some standard called "need" may be determined. If that is need, then we have no further problem. If, however, we expect the most intense desires of individuals to be fulfilled by reference to predetermined rules or by means of an adjudicated standard, then we are expecting a task from these techniques for social decision to which they are unsuited.

THE POLYCENTRIC PROBLEM

In our discussion thus far of the functional limits of legally controlled decision making, we have considered the necessity for decision-guides that contain the ingredients of rules and standards. There is a further situation that is unsuited to solution by the adjudicative process, because of the kind of problem it poses.

Fuller contends that only two kinds of questions can normally be solved through the judicial process without placing it under strain and without dispensing with the procedural restraints surrounding judicial determinations: "yes-no questions" (is the accused guilty? was there a breach of contract?) and "more-or-less questions" (how much should the plaintiff receive in damages?), or a combination of the two.[43] Another sort of question, termed by Michael Polanyi "polycentric,"[44] cannot successfully be solved by adjudication because meaningful participation by the litigants through proofs and arguments is virtually impossible.

Polycentric problems involve a complex network of relationships with interacting points of influence. Each decision communicates itself to other centers of decision, changing the conditions, so that a new basis must be found for the next decision.

As an example of the polycentric problem, Fuller cites the case of a wealthy lady who died in New York City, leaving a collection of paintings valued at millions and drawn from different periods, different nations, different schools of art. Her will bequeathed the collection to the Metropolitan Museum and the National Gallery "in equal shares" but prescribed no apportionment procedures. Here the problem lies in the fact that if we seek the best solution by a series of approximations, the movement of a single painting might entail a host of compensating adjustments in the allotment of the other paintings because the value of the new collection, in terms of its coherence as a collection, alters the value of the items remaining. The polycentric problem is thus like a spider's web: "Pull a strand here, and a complex pattern of adjustment runs through the whole web. Pull another strand from a different angle, and another complex pattern results."[45]

As Fuller points out, most problems are in some degree polycentric because their solution is likely in some way to change the basis upon which future decisions will be made. The decision to grant a welfare recipient a new bed, for example, will deplete the Welfare Department's resources and leave that much less available to future claimants. Caseworkers must develop a "sense" of the budget to avoid granting too generously in January lest the coffers be depleted in December. When a decision becomes sufficiently polycentric to threaten the integrity of decision by adjudication, then the matter cannot meaningfully be decided in this way. Urban-planning decisions constitute an example.

The concept of "advocacy planning" has been put forward as a way to improve the "level of rationality" of the planning process.[46] The proponents of advocacy planning urge the use of adversary proceedings and legal techniques, implying that the urban-planning process is somehow amenable to judicialization. Paul Davidoff, for example, draws the analogy between planning and decision making by adjudication, stating that:

Fair notice and hearings, production of supporting evidence, cross-examination, reasoned decision, are all means employed to arrive at relative truth: a just decision.[47]

We can well appreciate the process by which rational solutions are generated through the adversary dialectic made possible by "procedural due process." We have seen that the advocate planners in Madison Park were successful in helping to clarify issues and reveal preferences. They also succeeded in gaining some concessions for their clients from the BRA. To suggest too close an analogy between the urban-planning process and the judicial processes or to suggest that we should "fashion a system of law for planning,"[48] is to ignore certain fundamental aspects of the planning process that make it unsuited to "judicial" decision.

First, the structure of urban planning does not easily allow an independent impartial decision maker who could act in a capacity analogous to adjudicator. The nature of the process necessitates the drafting of proposals by officials with the resources and skills necessary to conduct the requisite survey, investigation, and evaluation.[49] The individuals affected might react negatively to these proposals. The official agency will then judge the merits of the claims against the merits of its plan. Thus far there has been nothing analogous to adjudication because no independent decision maker has scrutinized the plans. At the public hearing before the agency, the roles of both advocate and judge will be performed by the agency. Only at the hearing before the city council does the independent position of the council place it in a position to act as adjudicator,[50] but here the polycentric problem arises.

Suppose (to draw on the Madison Park urban renewal experience as an example) the advocate planners suggested that housing be built on a location that had been scheduled for an admixture of existing local businesses and a school. The problem is not merely public housing versus business and school; for if the housing were to be placed on the location, the entire plan would need readjustment. Where would the businesses be located? Would the school be abandoned, or placed elsewhere? What would happen to those who were displaced by the relocated businesses and schools? No proof or argument could be meaningfully presented here,[51] because the decision about housing is linked to many other decisions, necessitating readjustment of the entire scheme.

For planning issues to avoid polycentricity, the issues would have to present clear alternatives. In Madison Park they resolved themselves into a single "yes-no" question and two "more-or-less" questions: Should the space not taken up by the school be converted to use for low- and moderate-income housing? How many units should be constructed? How much rent constitutes low and moderate? It might have been possible for the city council to act as adjudicator, but here a further practical limitation arose: The council had power only to pronounce on the plan as a whole[52] —no "compromise" could be effected by order of the council, however many objections they might have had to specific provisions in the plan. In Madison Park the matter was settled—but it was settled "out of court."

THE ADMINISTRATIVE PROCESS: A SUGGESTED TYPOLOGY

The typology submitted here is the result of a desire to assess more accurately whether an administrative task is amenable to legal control. Certain tasks are not ideally amenable to control by rule or to decision by adjudication and can be effectively decided only where the decision maker retains a wide degree of discretion. Other tasks can be effectively decided only on the basis of individual or collective preferences. This typology will attempt to categorize tasks in the light of their suitability to control by legal techniques. It is heuristic and inevitably artificial. Hopefully it may organize our concepts of the role of law in the administrative process.

The literature on the federal administrative agencies classifies administrative tasks into those that involve "rule making" and those that involve "adjudication." In the examples of administrative tasks we have encountered thus far, the tasks are more varied than those two. Some administrative bodies run housing projects, others grant money. Some dispense rehabilitative services; others collect items as disparate as garbage, rents, taxes, and intelligence. The typology will attempt to classify the administrative process in a manner that more realistically reflects the variety of tasks that administrative decision makers perform.

The Administrative Process

Low discretion	High discretion

1. Dispute-Settlement Tasks

Adjudication	Allocation
	Conciliation

2. Managerial Tasks

"Pure" administration	Administrative
Administrative service	policy making

3. Rule-Making Tasks

Interpretation	Planning
Low Discretion	High Discretion

Discretion

Discretion here will refer to the room for decisional manoeuvre possessed by a decision maker. Discretion is rarely absolute, and rarely absent. It is a matter of degree, and ranges along a continuum between high and low.[53] The decision maker has a high degree of discretion when he is guided only by such vague standards as "public interest" and "fair and reasonable." Where his discretion is low, the decision maker is limited by rules that do not allow much scope for interpretation. For the moment, we might note that discretion may be constrained too by nonlegal factors, such as the amount of available resources, time, professional norms, and the political pressures to which the decision maker is (or perceives himself to be) subjected.

It should be pointed out that we are not referring here to

the discretion of any given body (commission, agency, etc.) but to discretion exercised at any time with respect to a particular task. For example, an organization might start out with high discretion to perform a particular task and may then proceed to impose a limit on its discretion by abiding by past decisions. Hart and Sacks refer to this as "discretion on a one-way ratchet."[56]

Tasks

Administrative tasks can be classified in the following manner: dispute-settlement, managerial, and rule making. This classification more accurately reflects what administrators do than the traditional adjudication-rule-making dichotomy.

Dispute-Settlement Tasks.

Dispute-settlement refers to a task that requires a decision as to the merits of two or more competing claims. The dispute settlor may have to decide between the claims of an organization (e.g., a Welfare Department) and an individual (e.g., a welfare recipient). The dispute might be between two individuals—one complaining about the other's behavior (e.g., a complainant and a respondent before the MCAD)—or might involve two individuals competing for an independent item (e.g., two persons competing for the allocation of a radio channel).

Dispute-settlement performed with a low degree of discretion (although some degree of discretion is almost always involved) is, as we have seen, adjudication in its ideal-typical form. The degree of discretion is low because the decision maker will be constrained by having to justify his decision by reference to principles, rules, or standards. This constraint in turn fosters procedures in which proofs and arguments are presented to an independent decision maker.

It is wrong, however, to view adjudication as the only method of dispute settlement. Conciliation, for example, is another. Conciliation (as performed by the MCAD) is a process in which the decision maker will attempt to reach a decision supported by the parties to the dispute. The task necessarily involves a high degree of discretion, both as to the terms of the decision and the process of arriving at that decision. During the process the conciliation officer has the power to propose concessions, adjustments, and compromises to the parties involved. The procedural restraints necessary to adjudication are thus absent because the decision maker often meets with the parties in private and has wide discretion to set flexible terms of settlement.[55]

It should be stressed again that these distinctions are artificially drawn here and that in practice they may merge. The distinction is however useful to place tasks that we have seen performed. For example, the determination of probable cause by the MCAD commissioner or the MCAD's task at a public hearing would be adjudicative. So would a welfare appeal referee's task in deciding whether a person was eligible for welfare, by reference to the relevant rule in the welfare manual. We have seen the strains placed upon adjudication when the appeal referee is required to decide the question of "special need' by adjudication. Because that decision requires a high degree of discretion, it is not ideally suited to adjudication, and proofs and arguments cannot be meaningfully presented. Such decisions would thus be placed higher on the discretion continuum, as the conditions for their resolution move away from those ideally required for adjudication.

Similarly, those who perform allocative tasks (disbursing limited resources among competing alternatives) normally possess a high degree of discretion. For example, the power of the Federal Communications Commission to issue licenses for the frequencies on the radio spectrum is guided by the vague standard of "public interest." Fuller's case of the art collection to be divided between two museums would be similar; being polycentric, its solution necessitates a high degree of discretion on the part of the decision maker.

The broad discretion in such determinations renders them unsuitable for adjudicative decision. Agencies performing allocative tasks may reduce their discretion by selecting narrower decision-making criteria, thus rendering the problem more suitable to decision by adjudication. For example, the "public interest" may be operationalized or factored into subgoals or criteria such as a "balanced program."

Managerial Tasks

Managerial tasks are oriented toward social goals.[56] The two kinds of managerial tasks that are placed at either end of the discretion continuum are "pure" administration and administrative policy making. It would be an error to assume that there is a distinct dichotomy between "policy" on the one hand and "administration" on the other.[57] Rather, "pure" administration and administrative policy making are functionally similar but situated at opposite ends of the discretion continuum.

"Pure" administration (or, in Ernst Freund's words, "administrative service"[58]) refers to the execution of largely routine service or regulatory tasks. It involves little choice of organizational objectives but does involve the strict "implementation" or "application" of policies already determined. As these tasks become less routine or mechanical, the discretion exercised in their performance increases, and they move along the discretion continuum towards administrative policy making, where the decision maker will make a choice about organizational goals and the means to pursue them.

For example, where a traffic patrolman follows instructions to allow traffic to pass along an intersection for two minutes from east to west and then for three minutes from north to south, he would be performing a purely administrative task. So little discretion is needed for this task that an automated traffic light may be used in place of a person. Where the patrolman has discretion to regulate traffic flow "as he sees fit" or "to maintain the free flow of traffic," he is exercising policy choices and performing a task unsuited to disposition by a traffic light.

A welfare intake worker, routinely deciding the eligibility of applicants on the basis of set qualifications (such as the age of 65 for Old Age Assistance) performs a purely administrative task. Where the caseworker made decisions about a recipient's "special need," the decision, as we have seen, requires a policy determination involving a high degree of discretion. These welfare decisions, however, are functionally distinct from the dispute-resolution tasks performed by a referee, who must assess the recipient's complaint about a caseworker's previous decision.

Rule-Making Tasks

An organization performs a rule-making task when it engages in the legislative process. The end product of the task will involve a rule, order, regulation, or plan. The process may be accompanied by various consultative techniques to obtain the views or participation of affected parties.

Rule-making performed with a low degree of discretion is referred to as "interpretative."[59] An agency makes interpretative rules when it "fills in the gaps" of clear policy, rules, or decision or specifies the means of procedure necessary for their application. As we have seen, rules that are supposedly "applied" are frequently elaborated and developed by the decision maker. Here the more elaboration involved, the farther the task along the discretion continuum. Examples of interpretative rule making would be the enactment of procedural requirements for the verification of illness or accident in welfare disability cases, or rules made by the

Securities Exchange Commission requiring the filing of notification of registration by investment companies.

Planning refers to the legislative task of devising a course of action that will effect an alteration in the public's state of affairs in accordance with the ends of an agency authorized to select those ends and the means for their attainment.[60] The urban renewal agency performs a planning task essentially legislative in nature, involving a wide degree of discretion as to the means to be employed to carry out its ends. Although we may not normally think of an urban renewal plan as a piece of legislation, the plan is in fact reduced to legislative form and will consist of a pattern of interlocking rules specifying the proposed alterations in a given area. Planning differs from allocation to the extent that the task does not involve a specific dispute-situation, but the designing of a course of action for the public as a whole. Once the plan is enacted, it remains to be implemented by a managerial process.

SUMMARY

This chapter has contended that the possibility (irrespective of the desirability) of subjecting official behavior to legal control depends to a great extent upon the task in question. Certain tasks may be suited to resolution by techniques that are wholly unsuited to the resolution of others. Some tasks are not ideally suited to resolution by adjudication because they necessitate decision according to a high degree of discretion and cannot be brought under the rubric of a rule or standard. Others are not so suited because they are polycentric in nature. The above typology seeks to illustrate these points and to suggest a categorization of tasks that necessitate performance with varying degrees of discretion.

Clearly *some* decision can be made about any question, and using any procedure. For example, the cooks in a college cafeteria could be required to submit their menu daily to a committee nominated by the faculty, and students could argue for or against English pudding, Danish pastry or American apple pie. But as Fuller suggests, if reality veers too far from the ideal the "integrity" of the system will be eroded, because the claimants, under the guise of the judicial format, will in effect be unable to find referents for their arguments, and will thus be joining issue in an "intellectual void."

It is suggested that an understanding of the necessary role of discretion in relation to the task to be performed (and in the light of the functional limits of legal decision making) ought to compel our admission that law cannot be "fashioned" to solve all social problems or to control all administrative decisions. To ignore these facts, and to proclaim a legal right or remedy where it is unsuited, will produce few benefits that are other than symbolic.

The Functional Limits of Legality

Notes

1. For a discussion of the difference between rules, principles, and policies (without distinguishing standards as used here), see R. Dworkin, "The Model of Rules," 35 *U.Chi. L. Rev.* 14 (1967); G. Hughes, "Rules, Policy and Decision Making," 77 *Yale L. J.* 411 (1968); L. Friedman, "Legal Rules and the Process of Social Change," 19 *Stan. L. Rev.* 786 (1967). For a distinction also of standards, see G. Gottlieb, *The Logic of Choice* (1968), and H. Hart and A. Sacks, *The Legal Process* (1958).

2. R. Pound, *Jurisprudence*, vol. 2, at 124 (1959).

3. See H. Hart and A. Sacks, *op. cit.*, at 155.

4. This position differs from that of Dworkin, *op. cit.*, who considers that a judge does not have discretion when he is bound to reach an understanding of what his orders or the rules require and to act on that understanding.

5. See generally Fuller's latest reply to Hart in *The Morality of Law*, chap. 5 (rev. ed., 1969).

6. See Nonet's account of the first stage of the California Industrial Accident Commission, where a claimant was seen as a "whole man," in the context of his work record, to judge whether he possessed a "reliable character" and to provide for his problems, family adjustment, physical and mental health, etc. P. Nonet, *Administrative Justice*, at 250-260 (1969).

7. For example, in the judgment of juvenile delinquent cases. See J. Handler, "The Juvenile Court and the Adversary System: Problems of Function and Form," *Wis. L. Rev.* 7 (1965).

8. J. Q. Wilson, *Varieties of Police Behavior*, at 65-66 (1968).

9. P. Freund, *The Supreme Court of the United States*, at 37 (1962).

10. See L. Fuller, *The Morality of Law*, at 64 (1964).

11. This apart from the question as to whether "immoral" conduct should be punished by a criminal remedy. See H. L. A. Hart, *Law, Liberty and Morality* (1963), and P. Devlin, *The Enforcement of Morals* (1965).

12. Murray v. Dunn (1907) A.C. 283.

13. See F. James, "The Qualities of the Reasonable Man in Negligence Cases," 16 *Missouri L. Rev.* 1 (1951).

14. H. L. A. Hart has pointed out that the standard by which "like" cases may be judged varies with the classification of the thing to which they are applied: "A tall child may be the same height as a short man, a warm winter the same temperature as a cold summer, and a fake diamond may be a genuine antique." H. L. A. Hart, *The Concept of Law*, at 156 (1961).

15. For a discussion of compensation in the context of property expropriation, see F. Michelman, "Property, Utility and Fairness: Comments on the Ethical Foundations of 'Just Compensation' Law," 80 *Harv. L. Rev.* 1165 (1967). Michelman considers that the concept of

"fairness" here "resists being cast into a simple, impersonal, easily stated formula," *ibid*., at 1250.

16. For an excellent discussion of the possible criteria of "desert" confronting the arbitrator attempting to establish a "fair rate" for a job, see S. Benn and R. Peters, *The Principles of Political Thought*, at 157-162 (1959).

17. H. Friendly, *The Federal Administrative Agencies: The Need for a Better Definition of Standards*, at 55-56 (1962).

18. "Midnight Welfare Searches and the Social Security Act," 72 *Yale L. J.* 1347 (1963); "The New Property," 73 *Yale L. J.* 733 (1964); "Individual Rights and Social Welfare: The Emerging Legal Issues," 74 *Yale L. J.* 1245 (1965).

19. For example, Shapiro v. Thompson, 394, U.S. 618 (1969) (Residence requirement held unconstitutional); Smith v. King, 88 S. Ct. 2128 (1968) ('man in the house' rule held unconstitutional); Goldberg v. Kelly 90 S. Ct. 1011 (1970) (hearing subsequent to termination of aid unconstitutional). See generally, F. Michelman, "Forword: On Protecting the Poor Through the Fourteenth Amendment," 83 *Harv. L. Rev.* 7 (1969); J. Graham, "Civil Liberties Problems in Welfare Administration," 43 *N.Y.U. Law Rev.* 836 (1968); "Social Welfare: An Emerging Doctrine of Statutory Entitlement," 44 *Notre Dame L Rev.* 603 (1969).

20. 74 *Yale L. J.* 1245, 1253 (1965); See also E. Sparer, "The Role of the Welfare Client's Lawyer," 12 *U.C.L.A. L. Rev.* 361 (1965), cf. J. Handler, "Controlling Official Behavior in Welfare Administration," 54 *Calif. L. Rev.* 479 (1966).

21. For the concept of need and wants adopted here see S. Benn and R. Peters, *The Principles of Political Thought* (1959). See also C. Bay, "Needs, Wants and Political Legitimacy," 1 *Canadian J. Poli. Sci.* 240, 242 (1968).

22. The "basic budgetary need" is designed to cover food, rent, fuel and utilities, household supplies, clothing, personal care, and life insurance, *Mass. Manual*, c. 4, § A, at 1-3.

23. The *Manual* lists some of these needs, namely, "nursing or housekeeping services and other special needs as laundry, household chores, telephone, special diet, etc., ..." The list is not considered exhaustive. *Mass. Manual*, c. 4, § A, p. 3.

24. A. Maslow, "A Theory of Human Motivation," 50 *Psychological Review*, 370 (1943); *Motivation and Personality* (1956).

25. For an account of this concept see W. Runciman, *Relative Deprivation and Social Justice* (1966).

26. J. Galbraith, *The Affluent Society* (1958).

27. *Ibid.*, chap. 11.

28. J. Keynes, *Essays in Persuasion*, at 365-366 (1952).

29. J. Galbraith, *op. cit.* Compare Marcuse's discussion of "true" and "false" needs. H. Marcuse, *One Dimensional Man* (1964). Banfield, in defining poverty, distinguishes "destitution," "want," "hardship,"

and "relative deprivation." He feels that the measure of poverty can only take into account the first two of these. E. Banfield, *The Unheavenly City*, at 16 (1970).

30. "While all wants are evaluated in terms of individual preference patterns, these patterns are not determined in a Robinson Crusoe setting." R. Musgrave, *The Theory of Public Finance*, at 11 (1959).

31. Cf. Banfield, *op. cit.*, at 117.

32. The response of the New York City Welfare Department to the flooding of requests for special need was to withdraw the discretion of caseworkers to provide extras and to provide instead a flat grant of $100 per year for extras. *New York Times*, Saturday, October 26, 1968, p. 1, col. 6.

33. See Boston *Globe*, Monday, September 2, 1968.

34. The goals of the Massachusetts program are defined generally as "achieving, to the extent possible, the objectives of stronger family life, social rehabilitation, self-care and economic independence for each individual family or adult." *Mass. Manual*, Introduction, and c. 5, p. 1.

35. *Mass. Manual*, c. 5.

36. The hearing referees may also be confronted with this problem. For example, one appellant claimed that the amount of an emergency grocery order should not be deducted from her monthly cheque. The referee upheld her claim on the ground that her initial excess expenditure was due to "personal inadequacy in budget management" and that the deduction "perpetuates her constant indebtedness and her inability to manage her funds."

37. 89th Congress, 2d Sess., Hearings Before the Senate Committee of Government Operations, "The Federal Role in Urban Affairs," pt. 6, at 1341 (1966).

38. See Boston *Globe*, Tuesday, November 19, 1968, p. 1, col. 1. Some of the specific abuses mentioned were the fact that in seven months a household furnishings store did $80,000 worth of business for welfare patients; one dentist grossed $164,000 in the same period, and a Boston taxicab company billed welfare for $47,862.05 for the first six months of 1968. Prescriptions for cosmetics, toothpaste, and bandages were written by doctors and paid for by welfare.

39. *Ibid.*

40. "Though what a man wants is not necessarily the same as what he needs, there is a *prima facie* case for treating his own view of what he needs with respect rather than giving him what somebody else thinks will be good for him." S. Benn and R. Peters, *op. cit.*

41. For the problems of measuring interpersonal utility, see K. Arrow, *Social Choice and Individual Values*, at 9 (1951).

42. H. Watts, "An Economic Definition of Poverty," in D. Moynihan, ed., *On Understanding Poverty*, at 322 (1969).

43. L. Fuller, "Collective Bargaining and the Arbitrator," *Wis. L. Rev.* i (1963).

44. M. Polanyi, *The Logic of Liberty*, 174-184 (1951). For an

excellent discussion of the polycentric problem, see P. Weiler, "Two Models of Judicial Decision-Making," *Can. Bar Rev.* 406 (1968).

45. Fuller, *op. cit.*, at 33.

46. The concept was first introduced by P. Davidoff, "Advocacy and Pluralism in Planning," 31 *J. Amer. Inst. Planners* 331 (1965). See also L. Peattie, "Reflections of an Advocate Planner," in E. Banfield, ed. *Urban Government*, at 556 (1969). See also C. Reich, "The Law of the Planned Society," 75 *Yale L.J.* 1227 (1966). Cf. L. Sullivan, "Administrative Procedure and the Advocatory Process in Urban Redevelopment," 45 *Calif. L. Rev.* 134 (1957).

47. Davidoff, *op. cit.*, at 332.

48. C. Reich, *op. cit.*, note 46, at 1233.

49. For a discussion of the planner's problems in initiating public discussion see A. Altshuler, *The City Planning Process*, chap. 5 (1965).

50. However, these hearings are generally considered "legislative," and not "judicial or quasi-judicial," thus precluding the right to cross examine and call witnesses, safeguards that are keystones of the advocate-planning and judicial processes. See Moskow v. Boston Redevelopment Authority, 349 Mass. 1213, 210 N.E. 2d 699, *Cert. denied* 282 U.S. 983 (1965).

51. See, e.g., "*Councillor William J. Foley*: I have never found a formula whereby we can look at relocation adequately at a hearing." *City Council Hearing on the South End, op. cit.*, at 650.

52. For example, "*Mr. Logue*: . . . you vote for or against the plan . . . you cannot amend the plan . . . legally it is the responsibility of the Boston Redevelopment Authority, and, in my view, not of yours to write the plan. . . ." *Ibid.* at 806-807. Cf: ". . . it is a physical and legal impossibility for us to change these plans, the only way the plans can be changed is for Mr. Logue to take the plans back and incorporate specifically what you people in Roxbury want." Councillor Langone, *Madison Campus High School Before the Committee on Urban Renewal*, November 16, 1966, p. 116.

53. K. C. Davis has recently defined discretion as follows: "A public officer has discretion whenever the effective limits on his power leave him free to make a choice among possible courses of action or inaction." K. C. Davis, *Discretionary Justice*, at 4 (1969). This definition views discretion as a matter of degree, and not as an activity distinct from "law-application," and accords with the view of discretion put forward here. Compare R. Pound, "Discretion, Dispensation and Mitigation: The Problem of the Individual Special Case," 35 *N.Y.U. L. Rev.* 925, 929-930 (1960). *Contra*, see R. Dworkin, "The Model of Rules," 35 *U. of Chi. L. Rev.* 14 (1967).

54. H. Hart and A. Sacks, *The Legal Process* (Tent. ed. 1958), at 160-180.

55. This particular form of conciliation differs from the usual form of mediation, which is categorized here as a purely administrative function, where the mediator only supervises a negotiated settlement, and the parties themselves are authorized to set its terms.

The Functional Limits of Legality

56. The distinction between managerial and dispute resolution is similar to that adopted by Selznick between "administration," the job of which is to "get the work of society done" and "adjudication," the primary function of which is to "discover the legal coordinates of a particular situation." Selznick, *op. cit.*, at 16.

57. See S. Simon, S. Smithburg, and V. Thompson, *Public Administration*, at 418 (1950).

58. E. Freund, *Administrative Powers over Persons and Property*, chap. 1 (1928).

59. For the various definitions of interpretative rules under the federal Administrative Procedure Act see A. Bonfield, "Some Tentative Thoughts on Public Participation in the Making of Interpretative Rules and General Statements of Policy under the A.P.A.," 23 *Admin. L. Rev.* 101, 108 (1971).

60. This definition is a synthesis of the definition of planning offered by M. Myerson and E. Banfield, *Politics, Planning and the Public Interest*, at 312-314 (1955); and J. Q. Wilson, "An Overview of Theories of Planned Change," in R. Morris, ed., *Centrally Planned Change*, at 13 (1964).

6

Discretion and the Politics of Administration

In the last chapter we concluded that substantive legalization or judicialization of administrative decision is not possible in a number of situations. The corollary of this proposition is that certain administrative tasks (those that cannot be performed by reference to rule or standard) require a degree of discretion for their effective exercise. What then (barring rules and standards) influences the exercise of this discretion? This question will be pursued in the present chapter. The answer will be sought through an examination of the operations of the MCAD. Such an examination will allow us to observe the administrative process over a period of time and to note the influences on the decisions. We shall then be in a position to evaluate the significance of influences on administrative decision making in terms of the possibility or desirability of controlling discretion by law.

DISCRETION AND THE ENFORCEMENT OF ANTIDISCRIMINATION LAWS

We have seen that uniformity (like treatment of like cases) is a quality sought by proponents of the legal control of administration. The essential finding of the following examination of the MCAD is that the results of the cases display a marked absence of uniformity.

The MCAD commissioners make decisions that are relatively free from legal constraints. We have seen that, after a finding of probable cause, the commissioners have the power to eliminate the discriminatory practice by means of an agreement arrived at after a process of conciliation.[1] Normally the conciliation agreements are settled by the investigating commissioner and the respondent alone, with the complainant having no say in the terms and no way to appeal terms of which he disapproves.[2] A recalcitrant respondent could pursue the matter through a public hearing. The commissioners' discretion is thus wide. Although the commission has the power to issue orders, after a public hearing, to "effectuate the purposes" of the act,[3] to make rules and regulations,[4] and to "formulate policies to effectuate the purposes" of the law,[5] it has rarely availed itself of these powers. No guidelines have been established indicating either the permissible range of the content of conciliation agreements or the variety of possible purposes (such as deterrence, rehabilitation of the respondent, general retribution, or remedy for the complainant) that the agreement might be expected to further. Nothing in the legislation enlightens us on the law's purposes.[6] The absence of formal legislative history makes it difficult to interpret the legislative purpose, especially because the original machinery, designed to deal with discrimination in employment alone, has been substantially retained to combat discrimination in housing and other areas.

Making use of these wide discretionary powers, the MCAD has developed in three stages since its inception, each relying on a different technique of enforcement. Although these stages are not clear-cut, and indeed overlap, having developed by a process of accretion rather than distinct elaboration, analysis of the history of the commission suggests that three different views of the purpose of the law, and of the appropriate role of the administrator, have been held. They may be characterized as follows:

1. "The primary object of the law is to eliminate racial discrimination in the community. The function of the

170

Commission is to persuade and educate members of the community to obey the law." This will be referred to as the "didactic" approach to the enforcement of the law. This term is borrowed from Henderson to describe one form of Japanese conciliation.[7] He describes "didactic conciliation" (as opposed to "prestate conciliation," or "voluntary conciliation") as "persuasive, educational, and instructive, it assists the authorities and the parties in achieving an understanding as to what is *required* of the alleged offender."[8]

2. "The primary object of the law is to vindicate the rights of individuals who have been the victims of unlawful discrimination. The function of the Commission is to adjudicate a dispute and protect the rights of the parties." This will be referred to as the "tort approach," because a complainant is viewed as a plaintiff in a civil action, suing the defendant for a civil wrong (tort) that violated the defendant's duty of care towards the plaintiff.

3. "The primary object of the law is to equalize opportunities for blacks. The function of the Commission is to remove obstacles to equal opportunity by eliminating discrimination that faces the complainant (and blacks generally in the community)." This will be referred to as the "equal opportunity" approach, because the complaint is viewed largely as a lever to reduce discriminating practices rather than to educate the respondent or to vindicate the strict legal rights of the complainant.

Stage One: The Didactic Approach

The first stage of the commission's history stretches from its inception in 1946 to approximately 1960. It will be suggested throughout this study that the patterns of administrative decision making are in many cases influenced by the political environment in which an organization is operating. The first stage of the MCAD's development can be explained by the political circumstances surrounding the passing of the original act and the subsequent political climate.[9]

171

In February 1945 several bills proposing antidiscrimination legislation were introduced in the Massachusetts House of Representatives.[10] The previous two years had witnessed nationwide racial riots and the outbreak of anti-Semitic vandalism. In December 1944 the Massachusetts House Committee on Labor and Industries reported the results of an exhaustive survey "on the matter of discrimination against persons in employment because of their race, creed, religion or nationality,"[11] and came to the conclusion that

in many directions there are practices of racial and religious discrimination in employment. Many leading institutions, public and private, even at this late date ... continue to require an applicant to answer questions which disclose religious affiliations or racial origin.... [Discrimination] is accomplished by so many devious and various means that no single corrective rule can be applied to prevent the injustices committed.[12]

The committee recommended "some legislation and appropriate machinery to protect those who are thus discriminated against."[13]

One of the bills drafted by Charles P. Curtis, Jr.,[14] a Boston lawyer, was modeled on the New York State Ives-Quinn Act[15] and proposed the creation of a state commission to administer a law outlawing discrimination in employment. Although the bill was "lobbied as no other bill has ever been lobbied in the Commonwealth before,"[16] it took 18 months and numerous setbacks and amendments to impel it into legislation on May 21, 1946,[17] in the face of powerful opposition.

The main opposition to the proposed legislation came from commercial and industrial interests. The Associated Industries of Massachusetts, the Boston Chamber of Commerce, and several real estate boards were prominent among them.[18] They opposed mainly on the ground that the legislation would be a "burden on business."[19] The executive committee of the Massachusetts Bar Association also expressed opposition, fearing a "new Governmental Bureau with inquisitorial powers . . . at a time when the public looks forward hopefully to less interference from government at the end of the war, and when Massachusetts needs to attract business to provide jobs for returning servicemen."[20]

One of the speeches made by a member of the Massachusetts House of Representatives, Representative Henry L. Shattuck, expresses a view common among the opponents of the legislation:

Before I discuss the proposed bill, I wish to make it clear that I am not here as an advocate of race prejudice. On the contrary, I have always believed that people should be accepted and judged according to their personal character and attainments, and not on the basis of race or creed. Some of my most valued friends are of the Jewish race. . . . The use of compulsion will intensify existing prejudices and will therefore defeat its purpose . . . like prohibition. . . . I therefore oppose a bill which in its practical effect gives power to an appointed commission to compel an employer to employ, or to promote, a person of a particular race or faith who is not acceptable to the employer.[21]

In response to statements such as these the bill's draftsman was at pains to point out that the new commission's "chief job will be *neither administration nor enforcement as such, but education and conciliation.*"[22]

The atmosphere surrounding the 1946 bill undoubtedly influenced the original enforcers of the law. It was a law passed as a result of a highly organized lobby campaign and aimed in good part at dispelling discrimination against Jews as well as blacks.[23] It was a law expressly claimed by its draftsman as relying on education and conciliation for its administration and enacted at a time of strong public and industry apprehension at "government coercion."

The first commission, appointed by the governor with the advice and consent of the senate, was likely to consist of individuals who appreciated the social and political factors surrounding the genesis of the law and would seek the support of those who opposed the bill most strongly— commerce and industry. An editorial advised on the choice of chairman and associate members: "Ardent crusaders might well be bypassed, for cool judgment, patience and tolerance, and a spirit of inquiry and compromise are the requisites, not a zeal for quick reforms and for exemplary penalties."[24]

The first annual report of the commission echoed these sentiments:

The Commission has approached the administration with a keen appreciation of the necessity of dealing fairly and peaceably with all parties who are subject to its provisions. It has not chosen to conduct a punitive expedition in Massachusetts but has preferred to steer a conservative course of educating employers and workers alike as to their responsibilities and obligations under the Law. The Commission has been continually mindful of this policy.[25]

The commission boasted that in one conciliated case the respondent wrote "how much the Company appreciates your intelligent, fair, and impartial manner in handling this case."[26] Finally, the commission related that many large business organizations had, on their own initiative, revised their employment policies, and "for this reason it is the feeling of the Commission that the very existence of the Fair Employment Practices Law had made our citizens conscious of their obligations to afford all parties an equal opportunity to work."[27] The following year the commission again stressed that "the existence of the law had awakened many employers to their obligations."[28]

At the outset, therefore, the commission saw its role as that of pursuing a "conservative course," relying mainly on "education," believing that the mere existence of the law would in itself eliminate discrimination, and anxious, above all, to obtain the good will of the business community.

In 1952 the commission checked the employment practices of 270 former respondent employers against whom complaints had been laid and conciliated during the three preceding years. The commission considered that its own policies were vindicated by the discovery of a 13-fold increase in minority group employment in 26 of these firms.[29] However, in a survey of 47 former respondent employers conducted in 1962, Mayhew concludes that there is no clear evidence to show that the employers regarded the law, or the commission, as "a serious threat or a powerful force."[30] In the responses from employers against whom probable cause had been found, Mayhew discovered that each considered that the case had not gone against him. One thought the case had been dismissed; another stated that if the case had gone against him, he would have taken it to court. All agreed that the commission was moderate, conciliatory, did not presume guilt, and treated them fairly.[31]

Mayhew's findings corroborate the fact that the first stage of the commission was "didactic." At the same time they expose the limitations of these policies. The commission, during this stage, conceived its methods to be those of persuasion and education ("reason not force");[32] it was also anxious to disprove the contention of the opponents of the law that the commission would provoke, not lessen, racial tension. However, a practical limitation arose when the same businessmen who were to be persuaded to cease their political opposition to the law confronted the commission as respondents: Because the commission's uppermost concern was appeasement of opposition, respondents were mollified rather than restrained in their actions.

Stage Two: The Tort Approach

Until 1960 it appears that the commissioners adopted a uniform approach along the lines suggested as characterizing the first "didactic" stage. After 1960 some of the commissioners seem to have adopted a view that accords more closely to the "tort approach." This change dates roughly from the passing in 1959 of the amendment prohibiting discrimination in private housing.[33]

In contrast with the controversy surrounding the passing

of the 1946 act, the 1959 bill (and others that expanded the commission's jurisdiction and remedies) passed with unanimous and bipartisan support.[34]

The change in the view of the law and of the commission's function was no doubt influenced by the change in public attitude and social conditions during the late 1950s and early 1960s.[35] Fair housing groups sponsored complaints to the commission[36] and watched their progress through every stage of the commission's procedure, often providing the complainants with counsel to press for their rights. Therefore, for the first time pressure was brought to bear on the commission from the complainant's side; at the same time the pressure from the respondent's side had eased. The commission was called upon to take its place in the line of civil rights organizations operating in the state.

Mayhew's survey bears out the suggestion that at this time at least some commissioners came to believe that the purpose of the law was to vindicate the rights of individual complainants and that the function of the commission was to enforce the rights of the parties. His survey shows that respondents in housing cases were more aware of the force of the law and the power of the commission.[37] In contrast to the respondent employers, respondents in housing cases found the commission "ominous, threatening and very salient."[38] The vast majority of respondents interviewed by Mayhew saw the law as operating against their interests and controlling their behavior. Clearly, emphasis had now shifted to vindication of the rights of the complainant rather than appeasement of the law's opponents. Whereas only two public hearings had been held by the commission from 1946 to 1960, two were held in 1961 alone, again demonstrating an added emphasis on the commission's adjudicatory role. In 1965 the commission successfully sponsored legislation that specifically authorized an award of damages to a complainant after a public hearing.[39]

Stage Three: The Equal Opportunity Approach

The third stage of the commission's development emerges from an analysis of the cases closed before one of the commissioners as discussed below. The commission seemed to move into this stage in the late 1960's.

This approach to enforcement sees a strong, affirmative purpose to the law. The goal is to remove barriers in the way of opportunities for blacks in the community. Individual cases that come to the commission are regarded as levers to be used to pry open and expose to scrutiny the respondent's entire range of operations. Where the respondent's racial patterns (in housing or jobs) show strong imbalances, with few blacks, this fact will be taken as circumstantial evidence of discrimination. The approach thus differs from the legalistic tort approach, where the direct liability of the respondent towards the complainant is the only point in issue.

The equal opportunity approach demands "affirmative action" from the respondent even if discrimination against the complainant is not demonstrated—for example, where the complainant is clearly unqualified for the job in question. Thus, even where the complaint is dismissed for lack of probable cause, or where the respondent moots the case by yielding on a specific apartment or job, the commission's access to the respondent's operations will be exploited. Consequently, the respondent might be required to widen his sources of recruitment to include black placement sources, to offer the next available job to a black, to lessen superfluous qualifications that might indirectly discriminate against blacks because of their relatively lower educational status, or to train blacks for certain skilled jobs.

The commission's 1965 annual report contained for the first time a policy statement asserting that

Aggressive affirmative action, as well as corrective action, is a necessary ingredient in our rapidly changing times.

... Positive, affirmative actions by the leadership of business, labor, public education, social agencies—all the institutions of our communities and government are necessary to achieve ... constructive social change.

We will attempt to improve the handling of individual complaints, intensify our own efforts in affirmative action and give leadership encouragement and expert assistance to any such efforts.[40]

THE DIVERGENCE OF GOALS AND OUTCOMES

An analysis of all the cases closed during 1965 shows that each of the commissioners was pursuing a different approach, coinciding with the three stages of the commission's development discussed immediately above. These three stages of growth were thus operating simultaneously. The reason is that the degree of discretion accorded the commissioners permitted each to impose his own view of the law's goals and his own means to achieve such goals through the cases brought before him.

Tables 6.1 and 6.2 display the absence, in 1965, of a uniform commission approach. Each commissioner has a different pattern of results. In order to evaluate the "success" of a case or group of cases, some criterion of success is necessary. One could be the complainant's success in obtaining the property or employment in question, another the respondent's future compliance. The reason for the wide variance in the results of the cases is that each commissioner has a different criterion of "success," depending on his view of the purpose of the law and of his function.

Table 6.1   Final Results of MCAD Housing Cases Closed before Commissioners A, B, and C, in 1965

Result	Commissioner A		Commissioner B		Commissioner C	
	Percentage	N	Percentage	N	Percentage	N
Complainants received relief	100.0	32	100.0	23	100.0	20
	78.1	25	69.5	16	90.0	18
Received the property	15.6	5	21.7	5	45.0	9
Refused the property offered	62.5	20	47.8	11	40.0	8
Received monetary compensation	0.0	0	0.0	0	5.0	1
Received no relief	21.9	7	30.5	7	10.0	2
Respondents complied or undertook compliance	100.0	35	100.0	24	100.0	18
	91.4	32	66.7	16	100.0	18
Gave complainant the property	14.2	5	20.8	5	44.4	8
Offered complainant the property	51.4	18	45.8	11	33.3	6
Undertook future compliance	60.0	20	8.3	2	38.8	7
Undertook affirmative action	8.5	3	8.3	2	16.6	3
Compliance checked by MCAD	2.8	1	0.0	0	33.3	6
Took no action	8.5	3	33.3	8	0.0	0

Table 6.2 Probable Cause Findings of MCAD Housing Cases before Commissioners A, B, and C, in 1965

Finding	Commissioner A		Commissioner B		Commissioner C	
	Percentage	N	Percentage	N	Percentage	N
Lack of probable cause	18.9	7	50.0	12	23.9	5
Settled after investigation and conference*	81.1	30	50.0	12	76.1	16
Finding of probable cause	18.9	7	37.5	9	61.9	13
No specific finding	62.2	23	12.5	3	14.2	3
Total	100.0	37	100.0	24	100.0	21

*Cases that are not dismissed for lack of probable cause are labeled in this manner. In some cases the case files indicate that a specific finding of probable cause has been made. Other cases show no evidence of such a finding.

Commissioner A: The Didactic Aproach

The procedures followed by Commissioner A typify the first stage of the development of the MCAD. Believing that the main aim of the law is to educate the community to eliminate discrimination, he regards his own function to be that of effecting "conciliation."[41] Commissioner A's cases show the following features:

1. A relatively low percentage of cases (15.6, compared with 21.7 and 45.0 for Commissioners B and C respectively) resulting in the complainant's receiving the desired accommodation. This demonstrates a relative lack of concern for the rights of the individual complainant, in contrast to the "tort approach."

2. In a relatively high number of cases (three in every five) the respondent indicated his intention to comply with the law in the future by writing the commission a letter to that effect. This too indicates that Commissioner A is mainly concerned with eliciting from the respondent some commitment to nondiscriminatory behavior in the future.

3. In only three cases did the respondent agree to undertake affirmative action. In two of these, the action was merely to place the commission's poster on view in the respondent's model home and rental agency. In the other complaint, brought by the MCAD, the respondent agreed to place a poster on display and to inform the commission of any future vacancies.

Thus Commissioner A, although eager to press for some commitment from the respondent, is reluctant to urge more than a minimum *negative* undertaking, such as a statement not to discriminate. Such reluctance also typifies the "didactic" approach where the commission's function is viewed as that of education and persuasion in order to encourage respondents to refrain from discrimination.

4. There were relatively few specific findings of probable cause or lack of probable cause. This, above all, distinguishes

the approach of Commissioner A from that of Commissioners B and C and is due to two reasons, each typifying the first-stage approach: first, Commissioner A is anxious to obtain the goodwill of respondents. In the absence of blatant evidence of discrimination, he is reluctant to put undue pressure on the respondents for fear of jeopardizing any goodwill that exists or might be induced on their part. He believes that a finding of probable cause would "antagonize" the respondent.[42] Second, Commissioner A sees himself less as an adjudicator of a dispute than as a negotiator on behalf of the commission. He is loathe to assign culpability at an early stage of the proceedings, for to do so, in his view, would imperil the satisfactory outcome of the case by either stiffening the respondent's resistance or placing an extra bargaining weapon in the hands of the complainant. The commissioner stated that he finds probable cause specifically only in cases where "they [respondents] give me enough trouble."[43]

Because he considers that his task is to obtain a commitment not to discriminate rather than to make a determination of right, Commissioner A is likely to ignore the letter of the law in order to reach what he considers to be its goal. Once a complaint has been laid, therefore, he will consider a case "satisfactorily adjusted" when the respondent indicates an intention not to discriminate in the future. Two interpretations could be placed on this method of resolving cases. First, no finding relating to probable cause has been made, and the commissioner proceeds immediately to conciliation. For example, one case was closed with the statement that "there has been a misunderstanding. Respondent has written a letter stating her policy of nondiscrimination." Second, in these cases the finding of probable cause is understood, or even presumed, from the complaint itself, and the burden of compliance or conciliation is placed upon the respondent, who can discharge this burden by indicating an intention to obey the law. This would explain an example where a respondent realtor had informed a complainant seeking a house in a new development that all the houses had been sold. An independent witness and the field representative produced evidence that the houses were in fact available. The case was closed after the respondent sent a letter indicating an intention not to discriminate and offered the complainant a house. The final written disposition indicates how the burden of compliance is placed upon the respondent. It stated that the complainant was "*allowed* to review the respondent's lists, and that the complainant *admits* to this 'red-carpet treatment.' "[44] The case was listed as "adjusted after investigation and conference," but no finding relating to probable cause had been made.[45]

In employment cases a similar pattern exists. On no occasion did Commissioner A make a specific finding of probable cause. Nevertheless, in two of the eight lack-of-probable-cause findings, the complainant had been offered the job in question, and in a third case the respondent had sent a letter of compliance. Again Commissioner A's cases indicated a concern with the respondent's professed intentions rather than with the complainant's rights or the opportunities for blacks in the community. For example, in one case the commissioner was satisfied with an indication of nondiscriminatory intent from the respondent without requiring that he offer the next available post to the highly qualified complainant. In no employment case did Commissioner A require affirmative action (e.g., the requirement that the respondent recruit black applicants) from the respondent.

Commissioner B: The Tort Approach

The following characteristics distinguish Commissioner B's cases:

1. The relatively high percentage of cases (one in three, as compared with one in twelve for Commissioner A) in which a case was closed without any action taken by the respondent.

Whereas Commissioner A is anxious to obtain from the respondent some commitment not to discriminate, Commissioner B sees his primary function as that of adjudicating the dispute between the complainant and the respondent. He will thus close a case upon finding a lack of probable cause, not being concerned with educating the respondent or regarding the complaint as a way of furthering opportunities for blacks. Similarly, upon finding probable cause, Commissioner B will seek a remedy closely related to the terms of the original complaint and a vindication of the rights of the complainant.

Many cases brought before Commissioner B demonstrate his prime concern with the rights of the complainant and an unwillingness to demand anything more of the respondent than action *toward the complainant*. The final disposition of one case, for example, reads: "Discrimination is clear and admitted. Respondent offered housing to complainant who declined it. Therefore this case is closed." No future compliance commitment was elicited from the respondent despite his clearly discriminatory behavior. In another case an owner of many apartments was not required to make any commitment to future compliance once his offer to the complainant was refused—even though the evidence of discrimination was blatant, the respondent having complained to the field representative of "the trouble the Niggers are causing."

2. In most cases a specific finding relating to probable cause. This again is because Commissioner B regards his function to be that of adjudicating a tort issue and is keen to make a clear determination of the rights of the parties.

3. In only two cases was affirmative action required of the respondent, and in no case was a commitment to future compliance required, again showing a prime concern with the parties to the dispute.

In employment cases too Commissioner B was on the whole unwilling either to request any action upon finding a lack of probable cause or to make the terms of the conciliation wider than the terms of the compliant,[46] even in cases where the respondent's firm was virtually segregated and his recruitment so designed as to exclude black placement sources or areas.

Commissioner C: The Equal Opportunity Approach

The results of cases brought before Commissioner C illustrate the third approach to the enforcement of the law. Commissioner C believes that the purpose of the law is to remove barriers that stand in the way of equal opportunity for blacks in the community.

The complainant is regarded by Commissioner C as more or less like a plaintiff in a class action, representing blacks in the community. The respondent will generally be required to take affirmative action not only toward the complainant but also toward blacks in the community in general.

Commissioner C's treatment of housing cases differs significantly from Commissioners A's and B's in one respect: In *every* case the respondent undertook in some way to comply with the law in the future. Unlike Commissioner A, however, Commissioner C virtually never obtained compliance letters from respondents. Rather, he required affirmative action; and then checked whether the respondents lived up to their promises.[47] Unlike Commissioner B, the action required by Commissioner C from the respondent was not only toward the complainant, nor was it wholly dependent upon a strict finding of probable cause. Unlike Commissioner A, Commissioner C considered the rights of the complainant to be relevant, and almost half of the complainants obtained the accommodation they sought (compared with just over one in six of Commissioner A's cases and one in five of Commissioner B's).

In employment cases, Commissioner C similarly shows relative success in obtaining a commitment to future compliance from the respondent. In two of every three of these cases the respondent undertook to comply with the law as a term of conciliation, or his conduct was checked where no finding of probable cause had been made. In one case, for example, although the complainant was not qualified for the job in question, the commissioner required the respondent to manifest his good faith by offering the next available job to a black.

POLITICS, POWER AND THE MCAD

What conclusions can we draw from the divergence in case outcomes and goals, between the three commissioners and over time? Should we see the divergences as problems to be solved? Ought we to insist that rules be enacted to specify the "correct" approach and the desired outcome? Ought we to institute checks on individual discretion in order to attain a uniform approach—over time or at any one time?

A satisfactory reply to these questions can be given only when we know *why* the divergence occurred. The reason for the differences between the three commissioners in 1965 is in a sense coincidence. The three commissioners represented different stages of the commission's history. Commissioner A was one of the original appointees to the commission in 1946. By habit or inclination he had retained his old techniques and approach. Commissioner C had been recently appointed and was pioneering a departure from the then dominant approach of Commissioner B.[48] Their divergences thus represented a cross section of the commission's history, during which it had evolved from the didactic to the tort to the equal opportunity approach. Naturally the change from one stage to another was not clear-cut and different approaches between all of the three commissioners was exceptional, although often at least one retained the approach that was dominant at the time of his appointment.

Why did the MCAD change over time in this way? First an administrative body such as the MCAD is itself involved in the elaboration of "purpose" to the law that gave it birth. The purposes of the law in this case were not clear; each of the three differing approaches was a logically acceptable reading of that purpose. Organizations such as the MCAD, therefore, cannot merely "mechanically" carry out their governing statute, as Weber's ideal-typical bureaucrat does; rather such organizations may be created for the expressed purpose of flexible task-performance, exercising a high degree of discretion. Weber's bureaucracy is as close to a machine as man can get. For some tasks machinelike impersonality and efficiency is welcome. In our society machines such as the parking meter and computer are actually usurping some of these. But other tasks are inherently unsuited to control by rules or standards. Decisions of welfare agencies about private needs, and of urban renewal agencies about public need, are cases in point. The task of conciliation similarly necessitates a high degree of discretion. In other situations, even though the task itself might be capable of relatively precise legal definition, the lawmakers might pass a vague mandate to the enforcing agency because of the inability to muster a majority in favor of a clearer standard. Legislative indefiniteness, in other words, may reflect a "political reason."[49] In still other situations, the legislature may grant a high degree of discretion to an agency specifically to achieve a flexibility for situations that cannot be perfectly anticipated.[50]

It should be remembered that public agencies are often unable to assess with accuracy the effectiveness of their operations. In the absence of an objective, ascertainable, or quantifiable criterion of "success," such as profit margin, ratings or productivity, organizations are frequently ignorant of how well they are doing. James Q. Wilson points out that no police department can know how much crime and disorder a community would suffer if the police functioned differently, or not at all.[51]

How do antidiscrimination commissioners evaluate the success of their operations—By the number of complaints they receive? By the amount of discrimination in the community? By the "strategic" nature of the complaints? Assuming any one of these criteria is selected, how is it measured? What is a "strategic" complaint? How do we know that discrimination is reduced, and how much of any reduction can we attribute to the commission's work? In welfare, too, goals are incapable of accurate measurement. How can we tell if a department is bringing recipients to a level of "self-support," or rehabilitating them?

Bureaucracies often respond to the problem of evaluating output by becoming "means oriented"; for example, judging the success of law enforcement by such criteria as the number of overall complaints, or judging the success of traffic enforcement by the number of traffic tickets issued.[52] Another way of measuring whether targets are being reached is to listen to those voices that are raised in support of or against the proposition that the organization is operating as it should.

The MCAD is therefore more than an elaborator of unclear standards. It does more than what organizational theorists refer to as the "factoring of goals into subgoals."[53] Peter Blau, for example, has described the "succession of goals" undertaken by agencies after they have achieved their original purposes and are induced by "irritating difficulties" to seek new organizational objectives.[54] Thus, Blau shows that, contrary to some views,[55] organizations do not necessarily resist change. They adapt to their environment in order to ensure their survival and, implicitly, the survival of the goals they are charged with furthering. Similarly, the change in case outcomes of the MCAD over time was not haphazard. Shifts in emphasis involved adaptation to its environment. The first stage reflected a response to strong opposition at a time when little organized support from civil rights groups was forthcoming. In the mid-1950s, overt opposition to the commission and the law abated, and pressure from complainants intensified. Perhaps the mode of enforcement in the first stage itself contributed to the abatement of opposition. In its third stage the MCAD seemed to find itself secure enough to act aggressively. In any event, the MCAD's actions can be attributed in large part to the way it evaluated its political options.

Bureaucracies are of course almost always structured so as to tie in to the political process. The BRA, for example, must obtain authorization for its plan from the city council. Most agencies depend upon the legislature for their appropriations and for the members' own reappointments. For example, many (including the author) believe that the welfare system should give more money to more poor people, that the MCAD should enforce the law more aggressively, in the manner of Commissioner C, that MCAD conciliation agreements should be tested and policed, and that the BRA should act more extensively to solicit greater participation from affected citizens. All of these measures, however, would most likely require additional funds for the three agencies. Higher grants for welfare recipients, more field investigators for initiating complaints and checking agreements, and more employees to monitor citizen desires would all require the authorization of additional expenditures by the legislative bodies consisting of elected representatives. The likelihood of these appropriations being forthcoming would then to a large extent depend upon the capacity of the agency to command public support, which will in turn depend upon its past actions and present friends.

This account of the MCAD shows that the lack of uniformity in administrative decision may well be quite functional. It may be possible to "legalize" or "judicialize" the MCAD's procedures, and to limit the divergences (over time and at any one time) by techniques that would minimize the scope of discretion. The advantage of rule-governed administration—such as evenhanded application and predictability—would then be achieved. The MCAD's flexibility, however, would be curtailed—perhaps at the expense of its capacity to adapt in order to survive and promote its objectives.

Notes

1. *Mass. Gen. Laws* c. 151B, s. 5.
2. At the time of this study the complainant had no recourse of appeal from a determination of lack of probable cause. He may now appeal to the full commission, *Mass. Act of 1967*, c. 483. However, the complainant may not appeal the terms of a conciliation agreement.
3. *Ibid.*
4. *Ibid.*, s. 3(5).
5. *Ibid.*, s. 2.
6. The first section of the original statute stated: "The right to work without discrimination because of race, color, religious creed, national origin or ancestry is hereby declared to be a right and privilege of the inhabitants of the commonwealth." *Mass. Acts of 1946*, c. 368, s. 1; amended by *Mass. Acts of 1950*, c. 479.
7. D. Henderson, *Conciliation and Japanese Law*, at 4 (1965).
8. *Ibid.*, at 5 (emphasis in original). See also J. Cohen, "Chinese Mediation on the Eve of Modernization," 54 *Calif. L. Rev.* 1201, 1224-1225 (1966).
9. See generally, L. Mayhew, *Law and Equal Opportunity* (1968). Again, this work will be drawn upon, but, where possible, material presented there will not be repeated here.
10. Boston *Herald*, February 16, 1945, p. 1, col. 1. Other laws had previously been passed, e.g., outlawing discrimination on the grounds of race, color or national origin in the state government or a subsidized street railway company. *Mass. Acts of 1920*, c. 376. See also *Mass. Acts of 1865*, c. 277, making discrimination in public places a criminal offense.
11. Mass. H. No. 337 (1944).
12. *Ibid.*, at 2.
13. Mayhew, *op. cit.*, mentions other committees (though not this one), such as the Massachusetts Committee on Racial and Religious Understanding, created by Governor Saltonstall in 1943 and empowered to conduct investigations and programs designed to combat discrimination. Two of the members were Mildred Mahoney and Mr. A. K. Cohen, two of the original commissioners on the 1946 Fair Employment Practices Commission (as it was then called).
14. Documents in the *Henry L. Shattuck Collection*, Littauer Library, Harvard, shows that Curtis' bill (Mass. H. No. 1934, 1945) was considered by the Mass. House of Representatives in February, 1945. Mayhew, *op. cit.*, at 79 suggests that a bill submitted by the New England Division of the American Jewish Congress was debated. Such a bill was submitted (Mass. H. No. 609, 1945) but not debated. Other bills submitted but not debated include Mass. H. Nos. 337, 436, 544, 162, 106 (1945). The bill was referred to by the Executive Committee of the Mass. Bar Association as the "Curtis Bill." The Committee opposed the bill. [See "Statement of Members of the Executive

Committee in Regard to the Pending Anti-Discrimination Bills," 30 *Mass. L. Q.*, 10 (1945).]

15. See "Memorandum by Charles P. Curtis, Jr., on the Anti-Discrimination Bill Submitted on Behalf of the Committee for a Massachusetts Fair Employment Practices Law to the Legislative Committee on State Administration," in the *Henry L. Shattuck Collection, op. cit.*, and a letter therein from Curtis to Shattuck dated March 22, 1945, describing the bill as "substantially the New York act adapted to Massachusetts procedures." For a history of the "Ives-Quinn Act," see L. Ruchames, *Race, Jobs and Politics* (1953), and M. Berger, *Equality by Statute* (1952).

16. Henry R. Silverman, "How We Won in Massachusetts," *New Republic*, July 8, 1946, p. 10.

17. *Mass. Acts of 1946*, c. 368.

18. H. Silverman, *op. cit.*. The supporters of the legislation included the American Jewish Congress, heads of Catholic and Protestant churches, the CIO, the League of Women Voters, the Democratic Party, and some "progressive members of business and industry."

19. Boston *Herald*, February 7, 1946, p. 1, col. 6.

20. 30 *Mass. L. Q.* 11, (1945).

21. This speech is written in full in the *Henry L. Shattuck Collection, op. cit.*, and was presumably delivered, as parts of it are quoted in the Boston *Herald*, June 21, 1945, p. 1, col. 1.

22. Memorandum by Charles P. Curtis, Jr., "To the Legislative Commission on State Administration," *op. cit.*, at 2 (emphasis added). Similar arguments were employed to overcome opposition to similar proposed legislation in England. For example, "much of the resistance should disappear when it becomes generally understood that legislation doesn't mean that every act of discrimination will be treated as a criminal offence—but that the law will simply be used as an ultimate sanction if the machinery of conciliation and persuasion doesn't work." *The Observer*, April 23, 1967, p. 12, col. 1.

23. The bill was referred to in the State House as "the Jewish Bill," Boston *Herald*, June 21, 1945, p. 1, col. 2. Collins, *State Regulation of Discrimination* Ph.D. thesis, Harvard University, at 419, writing in 1952, considers "the most striking fact" of the first four years of the existence of the New York State and Massachusetts Commissions was that 76% of the complaints were laid on the grounds of race and color. See also Representative Shattuck's speech, *op. cit.* The Massachusetts House Committee on Labor and Industries report seemed as much concerned with religious as with racial discrimination. Finally, the need for the legislation was impelled to a great extent by the anti-Semitic outbreaks during 1944 and, surely, an awareness of Hitler's anti-Semitic policies.

24. Undated and unidentified editorial in the *Henry L. Shattuck Collection, op. cit.*

25. Commonwealth of Massachusetts, *Fair Employment Practices Commission, Annual Report*, December 1946, p. 1.

26. *Ibid.*, at 7.

27. *Ibid.*, at 10.

28. Commonwealth of Massachusetts, *Fair Employment Practices Commission, Annual Report*, November 1947, p. 2.

29. *MCAD, Annual Report*, December 1952, pp. 9-10.

30. Mayhew, *op. cit.*, at 248.

31. *Ibid.*, at 247.

32. Commonwealth of Massachusetts, *Fair Employment Practices Commission, Annual Report*, November 1947, at 2. For instances of a similar approach carried out by the New York State Commission Against Discrimination, see M. Berger, *Equality By Statute*, chap. 4 (1952).

33. *Mass. Acts of 1959*, c. 239. The constitutionality of this amendment was upheld in MCAD v. Colangelo, 344 Mass. 387, 182 N.E. 2d 595 (1962). See Kozol, "The Massachusetts Fair Housing Practices Laws," 45 *Mass. L. Q.* 305 (1962).

34. See Mayhew, *op. cit.*, 91-100. Some of these amendments were: to prohibit discrimination in the granting of mortgage loans, *Mass. Acts of 1960*, c. 163; to provide for the suspension or revocation of the license of a real estate broker or salesman who failed to comply with an order of the commission, *Mass. Acts of 1959*, c. 181; and a provision to allow the commission to apply for an injunction to restrain the disposition of property or employment subject to dispute before the commission, *Mass. Acts of 1961*, c. 570. Amendments made before that time expanded the jurisdiction to include: public housing projects, *Mass. Acts of 1950*, c. 697; discrimination on the grounds of age, *Mass. Acts of 1956*, c. 426; educational institutions, *Mass. Acts of 1956*, c. 334; and "publicly assisted housing" (financed by FHA or similarly guaranteed loans on housing constructed under the urban redevelopment laws, *Mass. Gen. Laws*, c. 21A, *Mass. Acts of 1957*, c. 426.) Most of these earlier amendments were largely enacted as necessary preconditions to the receipt of federal assistance under the relevant programs.

35. Revealed, e.g., in the lack of opposition to the housing amendments in 1959 and in the improvement of employment opportunities for blacks.

36. Mass. Advisory Committee to the U.S. Commission on Civil Rights, *op. cit.*, at 54.

37. Mayhew, *op. cit.*, at 249.

38. *Ibid.*

39. *Mass. Acts of 1965*, c. 569. Damage not to exceed $1000, nor to include attorney's fees.

40. MCAD, *Annual Report*, January 1, 1965, to December 31. 1965, p. 4.

41. All the opinions expressed hereafter are culled from interviews with the commissioners and analyses of the cases. It should be remembered that the tabulations presented in Tables 6.1 and 6.2 reflect small numbers, so that care should be taken in drawing inferences of

statistical significance. The tabulations taken together, however, show a definite pattern.

42. Interview with Commissioner A.

43. *Ibid.*

44. Emphasis added.

45. The written "final disposition" sheet of these cases lists them under the abbreviation "A.I.C." Cases like those of Commissioners B and C, where such a disposition, with no probable cause finding, has been made, usually involve immediate capitulation by the respondent.

46. In one case, however, Commissioner B called an informal conference to work out methods of broadening the respondent's sources of recruitment to include black sources. In another case the respondent wrote voluntarily indicating his intention to comply in the future and that he was a member of the Massachusetts Plan for Progress, a scheme to provide job opportunities to minorities.

47. For example, "A follow-up revealed that Negro home-seekers were given most courteous treatment."

48. There was evidence that the commissioner who was replaced by Commissioner C followed Commissioner B's "tort" approach. Commissioner B was the chairman at the time of this study, and the field representatives and the staff were imbued with his conception of the law's goals. The chairman was replaced shortly after this study was completed. Commissioner C was pleased with the approach of his replacement.

49. W. Leys, "Ethics and Administrative Discretion," 3 *Pub. Admin. Rev.*, at 14 (1943).

50. See H. L. A. Hart on the two handicaps to advance regulation of human conduct—relative ignorance of fact and relative indeterminancy of aim [*The Concept of Law*, at 125 (1969)]. See also H. Simon's discussion on the limits on human rationality in decision, H. Simon, *Administrative Behavior*, chap. 5 (1945), and the discussion on the "cognitive limits of rationality" in J. March and H. Simon, *Organizations*, chap. 6 (1958).

51. J. W. Wilson, *Varieties of Police Behavior*, chap. 3 (1968). See also A. Downs, *Inside Bureaucracy*, chap. 3 (1967).

52. *Ibid.*, at 86.

53. See V. Thompson, *Modern Organization*, at 14-18 (1961).

54. P. Blau, *The Dynamics of Bureaucracy*, at 241 (1955).

55. See, e.g., R. Merton, "Bureaucratic Structure and Personality," in R. Merton, ed., *Reader in Bureaucracy* (1952). Nonet's study of the California Industrial Accident Commission shows a change in approach over the years: *Administrative Justice* (1969). See also M. Bernstein, *Regulating Business by Independent Commission* (1955), for an account of the "life cycle" of the Federal Regulatory Commission.

7

Legality, Advocacy, and Bureaucracy

We began this study with a discussion of the merits and defects of law to control administrative discretion. We discovered that legal techniques often contain mixed blessings and that their benefits from the bureaucracy's perspective were frequently offset by their burdens from the perspective of some or all of the bureaucracy's clientele.

We saw that rules could provide relative uniformity of application and certainty of expectation. Rules could encourage administrative integrity by inhibiting the use of arbitrary or improper criteria and by promoting a critical attitude to a law's content and to the manner of its enforcement. From the administrator's point of view rules could encourage planning and routinization. They allow for the conservation of energy, which would otherwise be expended on the constant reexamination of each case, and provide a welcomed shield from political pressures.

On the other hand, the existence of a rule does not guarantee the quality, fairness, or generosity of its content. Indeed, the seeker of "individualized" justice may resent being placed in a category that shields decision makers from considering unique individual circumstances. The by-product of certainty and uniformity is frequently legalism and rigidity.

195

The principal merit of adjudication, from the perspective of the litigant, is that it guarantees participation in the decision-making process and allows adversary challenge. The requirement of a reasoned justification for a decision will also promote public scrutiny and official accountability.

On the other hand, appeals to "legality" might in practice prove esoteric and mystical to claimants and the adversary situation might itself contain costs, particularly to a person challenging the decision of an official with whom he has an ongoing relationship. Adjudication is also a relatively ineffective planning technique because it is geared to the resolution of individual disputes and does not normally allow consultation with wider interests.

How do we resolve the respective merits and defects of legal techniques to control bureaucracy? Like others in favor of legal techniques, this author is committed to what Selznick calls the "ideal of due process"[1] as a desirable component of all public decision-making tasks. This ideal would allow a proper regard for all affected interests and would ensure decisions that affirm reason, are based upon a reliable assessment of fact, and are made with due regard to a person's basic minimum rights of personality. Other things being equal, official discretion ought to be limited, and persons affected by a bureaucracy's operations ought to be allowed the right to participate in decisions that will affect them and to challenge decisions that have done so.

The first qualification, however, is that things are not always equal and that, as we have seen, legal techniques to control bureaucracy do contain costs that ought to be weighed against the benefits.

The second qualification is that the nature of the task frequently decides for us whether, or to what extent, official discretion can be limited. We have seen that some problems (e.g., private need in welfare or public need in urban planning) are inherently unsuited to resolution by reference to rule or standard. Other tasks (e.g., conciliation or many allocative tasks) may require a high degree of discretion. It

196

has been suggested here that an analysis of tasks more sensitive than the traditional rule-making-adjudication classification is necessary in order to determine the necessary degree of discretion.

The third qualification, which we observed in connection with the operations of the MCAD, involves a recognition that administrative agencies are frequently participants in the development and elaboration of a law's purpose and that a major constraint upon their decisions is political acceptability. Thus in attempting to resolve whether public decision makers as a whole tend to act in a rule-bound fashion, in a manner that has been referred to as "bureaupathological,"[2] or whether they tend to proceed "thematically" and "incrementally,"[3] both the nature of the task and the perception of the political environment will determine the degree to which an organization will restrict its own discretion.

Most administrative bodies operate in a political arena and, like military bodies, would find rules permitting only conventional warfare restrictive when a flexible response or guerilla tactic is called for. The tactics of the typical regulatory agency consist of the "raised eyebrow," subtle threats and cajolement, and selective enforcement rather than the bludgeon blow of strict enforcement according to defined rights and firm obligations. In short, rules might perpetuate administrative action that was once appropriate but is no longer acceptable. Where the administrative response to this shifting situation is constrained by a rule, the organization in question is, at least, likely to lose legitimacy in the eyes of affected interests. At worst, because of its connection to the political process, it will lose its life.

A fourth qualification to the preference for the ideal of due process has received a good deal of attention in this study. It rests upon the need to recognize that access to law and bureaucracy is frequently limited. It should be stressed that this qualification, like the others, does not argue against the control of discretion through law but rather points to a limit to that control, which ought to be recognized because it may in fact inhibit the utilization of institutional mechanisms of control either generally or among certain groups.

In our examination of the welfare appeal we saw that many factors may inhibit complaints about official decision. Although the welfare situation may be atypical in some respects, it was shown that knowledge, attitudes, resources, and relationships must be taken into account as potential obstacles to the pursuance of channels of complaint. Our observation of complaints to the MCAD underlined some of these obstacles and suggested their relatively greater prevalence among low-status groups.

The question of access in regard to consultative rule-making procedures was considered through our examination of the limits to citizen participation in urban renewal. We observed that the possibility of access of certain individuals to an urban renewal agency is seriously limited—even where the onus of initiation appears to be on the agency. Effective participation generally requires middle-class verbal skills, a requirement emphasized when the main mechanism for participation is the public hearing. In Madison Park we discovered that many people were unable either to involve themselves in any aspect of community affairs or to participate in community or governmental organizations. Feelings of skepticism, hostility, lack of interest, or being overwhelmed by personal problems all contributed to this lack of desire, or incapacity, to attend a forum such as a public hearing or even to take advantage of administrative availability or consultation. The most genuinely open rule-making procedures are thus of limited value in soliciting the opinions, at least through conventional channels, of many individuals, particularly the poor and the unorganized.

How do we assess the significance of these four qualifications to the attainment of the "ideal of due process" in administration? The first three qualifications admit of no further conclusion here except that an acknowledgement of their existence will allow a more sensitive assessment of the possibility of submitting administrative discretion to control through law. The costs of legal control as well as the benefits ought to be weighed, and the limits of legal techniques and the politics of administration ought to be recognized.

Our fourth qualification, the problem of access, does give cause for concern. First, obstacles to access among certain groups might inhibit the achievement of organizational objectives (e.g., where "strategic" complaints about race discrimination are rarely laid). Second, where only certain groups are deterred from access, the result must be weighed by standards of social justice. Third, the mere existence of formal channels does not itself ensure democratic decision making. Rule-making procedures, for example, ideally allow consultation of affected interests and an implicit assurance that the rules will substantially reflect the merits of the arguments presented. In practice, however, rule-making procedures frequently amount to what Murray Edelman calls "symbolic reassurance"[4]—a technique whereby the myths, rituals, and symbols surrounding the state are invoked in order to achieve the "quiescence" of mass publics. In other words, rule-making procedures may be used by an administrative agency to give an impression of participation, whereas no more than *pro forma* adherence to an empty democratic ritual was involved.

Edelman's thesis assumes that symbolic reassurance is a typical administrative technique, borne of a functional necessity for the survival of an organization and the propagation of its aims. It is not necessary for our present purpose to test the validity of that thesis. We have already seen that ideally, the rule-making process could be enormously beneficial to an organization and its clientele. The open rule-making process is limited, however, in its ability to take certain interests into account, even where the opportunity for consultation was provided.

Concern also arises from the inevitably political nature of the administrative process. Limits to access to formal channels will probably apply with equal force to access to the informal and political processes. James Q. Wilson has noted that the "problem of the powerless"[5] is basically a problem of bargaining, where the powerless group seeks through protest to increase its stock of political resources to exchange. These resources are similar to those that allow for access to formal channels of participation, namely, access to information, money, established techniques of participation, and a high sense of political efficacy. The lack of these resources inhibits the exercise of influence upon the politico-administrative process as effectively as it inhibits access to formal channels of protest or consultation.

How can the opportunity of access to bureaucracy be equalized in fact? Instead of looking solely to legal techniques of decision to control official discretion, another legal device ought to be considered—namely, representation by advocates. Advocacy in an administrative setting, however, will be successful only if the advocates appreciate that the analogy between administrative and judicial decision making is loosely drawn, that political power is frequently an important ingredient of influence, and that certain administrative tasks cannot be molded into judically formulated "either-or," "more-or-less," "yes-or-no" questions.

ADVOCACY AND ACCESS

Advocates representing complainants in situations such as a welfare appeal hearing or an MCAD complaint would probably improve their clients' chance of winning through their knowledge of the law, familiarity with the procedures, and skill in persuasion.

One in five welfare appellants who appealed at the district office during the year was represented by the Mothers for Adequate Welfare (MAWS), sometimes aided by a lawyer from the Boston Legal Aid Society. The MAWS was formed in 1963 and was committed to the redress of a number of grievances, including the lack of access to the rules and regulations, lack of day-care centers, the requirement of a year's residency for receiving aid, and the necessity for support actions against deserting husbands. The MAWS also wanted a say in the policy-making process and the right to more generous "special need" than was provided.

In representing appellants, the MAWS or the lawyer would forcefully present the appellant's case,[6] frequently citing precedents. The lawyer would normally check the overall accuracy of his client's budget and ensure that his client was receiving items that were available but that the caseworker had not brought to her attention.[7]

The possibility of a client being represented would tend, therefore, to cause the caseworkers to be both more helpful and more scrupulously correct in their administrative tasks. For example, in about five instances caseworkers had capitulated to their clients' requests only after the client had threatened to invoke the help of the MAWS. In addition, both the caseworker and the referee would be prompted to be well informed of the facts of a case due for a hearing; the law would be more likely to be followed, and irrelevant prejudicial evidence or remarks less likely to be allowed.

In addition to overcoming the lack of technical skill among appellants, it is possible that the MAWS were succeeding too in overcoming some of the obstacles to access that we have discussed. First, the appellant would not herself encounter the caseworker as an adversary—a situation that we have seen might discourage appeals. The advocate and the caseworker would exchange any ill will that might be generated. Second, the MAWS' activity (highlighted by well-publicized demonstrations) affected the atmosphere of welfare appeals, making welfare seem like an entitlement, to be aggressively pursued, and not a privilege to be passively received.[8]

Similar findings apply to the experience of the MCAD. Of the 85 housing cases closed by the MCAD during the year, 45 were referred to the MCAD by Fair Housing, Inc., a Boston organization providing a housing service to families faced with race discrimination. Thirty-one of the 45 cases referred by Fair Housing were accompanied by an affidavit from a witness. Fair Housing, Inc., would normally follow the progress of a complaint throughout, arrange for the complainant to obtain the free services of a lawyer and, if called upon to do so, assist with the investigation.

The record of cases referred to the MCAD by Fair Housing, Inc. shows that it had no more "success" than other sources. In practice, however, Fair Housing Inc. could be considered more successful because it would probably refer a complaint for filing more readily than an individual who, for the reasons discussed above, would normally tend to file only when the case is clear-cut and easy to prove. Because Fair Housing, Inc., is able to test a case and provide a witness who would otherwise probably not be available, it is likely to provide the complainant with a stronger remedy than he would obtain on his own.

Fair Housing, Inc.'s aid was thus likely to ensure that a case of discrimination, which might otherwise go unchallenged, would be brought to the MCAD and to increase the chance of "success" of these cases. In addition, complaints referred by Fair Housing were distinguished by the fact that they normally alleged discrimination in an area of strategic importance for the integration of blacks in the community[9] because it was their policy to ignore complaints laid in an area where the "tipping point" had been reached and a formerly mixed area was tending to become all black.[10]

We have examined the role of the advocate planners in the urban renewal situation. Here too it can be assumed that Urban Planning Aid provided local groups with access to officials that they otherwise would not have had. It should, however, be made clear that even access perfectly and equitably achieved will not in itself ensure that proposals advanced will be reflected in the ultimate decision. Decision makers may themselves use mechanisms such as public hearings in order to enhance their own legitimacy and to provide "symbolic reassurance" that the democratic rules of the game have been followed. The public may be politely heard but promptly ignored. For example, Gans' study of a suburban community found that urban planners "decided how to vote before the public hearing, and simply sat through it as a legal requirement."[11]

In such cases the role of the advocate becomes more expressly political as he attempts to increase the power of his clients, thus decreasing the likelihood of their claims being ignored.

The mere intervention of advocates will at times do much to neutralize some of the most serious disabilities of groups by providing them with political and planning skills.[12] In the urban renewal situation, for example, we have seen that an agency's professional full-time staff and resources equip it, or appear to equip it, with an unrivaled competence to determine the public interest. The advocate's intervention could undercut the agency's monopoly of such skills. Logue shrewdly countered the challenge to his expertise on the part of advocate planners by dubbing them "semiprofessionals" and "academic amateurs."

In some cases, however, the advocate's intervention might in fact diminish his client's influence through the loss of an important asset—the persuasiveness and authenticity of an individual's pleading his own cause. Logue recognized this fact too when he taunted the advocate planners as being from "across the river" using their clients as "tinker toys of MIT and Brandeis." The influence of the advocate could, therefore, be said to equal the influence of the client plus the advocate's political and planning skills minus his lack of authenticity. This problem does not arise where the advocates are themselves members of the affected interest group, as in the case of the MAWS, although the advocate's "representativeness" could still be questioned.

In suggesting that the power of interest groups could be increased by advocacy, it is important to remember that power is not a "zero-sum" phenomenon.[13] The gain in power by A does not necessarily mean a decrease for B. The skills of the advocate could prove of particularly high value, therefore, if he were employed in seeking a solution that could achieve his client's wants without detracting from the goals of the agency, thus helping to achieve an optimal solution in terms of his client's and the agency's "self-regarding" ends.[14] The advocate planner would here act as coordinator, keeping track of internal economies and diseconomies, watching for "saddle points," offering positive as well as negative inducements to bargain and generally seeking to improve his client's position without necessarily threatening the power of the agency. By skillful negotiation, the advocate could make his client better off without anyone else necessarily being worse off. For example, the advocate could devise an alternative location for a proposed highway that would avoid the dislocation of his clients' neighborhood and save the agency money. In welfare, proposals for the abolition of routine investigations would similarly save the department money and would allow caseworkers to devote their time to other tasks. The model employed by the advocate of interest groups seeking to gain benefits from bureaucracy should thus not automatically be that of the lawyer in the traditional courtroom setting, where issues are congealed into "either-or" questions. Although there may be occasions where "confrontation" tactics are appropriate (if only to maintain the cohesion and solidarity of the advocate's client group), the advocate should be sufficiently flexible to use indirect routes of access, including pressure on public opinion, and to strike bargains and reach optimum settlements "out of court."

We should not assume that the interests of local "communities" are singular, that people on account of their social and economic situation necessarily share political views, or that the availability of advocates will of itself involve those who are reluctant or unable to participate. The LRCC was known to few residents of Madison Park. A community leader admitted to the BRA at a public hearing that neither he nor his organization was necessarily representative of the people for whom they claimed to speak; most were "apathetic and indifferent until things hit home." Advocates in this situation have two choices: They can attempt to mobilize the expression of community desires in the manner of community organizers such as Saul Alinsky.[15] This kind of mobilization is likely to be most successful when centered on parochial issues or immediate threats. We have seen in Madison Park that the most vociferous opposition came from persons whose own homes, churches, or businesses would be affected by the urban renewal plan. The MAWS were unsuccessful until they mobilized welfare recipients around the issue of personal material reward, namely, higher and more easily available special grants. Or, alternatively, the advocate could pursue the course suggested recently by one of the advocate planners in Madison Park:

I began to see that . . . the organization would be less effective if it continually had to incorporate, and assimilate into its internal processes, many members. What the organization needed to be effective as a political force was a limited group of leaders, enough supporters to fill a hall at occasional public meetings, and the absence of local opposition.[16]

Clearly representatives (or alleged representatives) of local groups cannot be faulted for utilizing political tactics such as the filling of halls in order to give the impression of mass public support. The state in our political culture continually manipulates the "quiescence"[17] of its mass public by devices such as public hearings, the show of telegrams of support, and other means of making the public believe that the democratic rules of the game are followed, that the official position is widely supported, and that a "unitary" concept of the public interest exists. Norton Long has remarked that an administrative agency deprived of power is "an object of contempt to its enemies and of despair to its friends."[18] The same could be said of those who do not comprehend the place of power and politics in administration or the effective methods of wielding power.

A final *caveat* is necessary: Even where an organization or individual could be considered "representative" of a majority of the affected population, traditional rule-making processes offer no way to order preferences. The views that are voiced will mostly propose the adoption of special interests, which might arise from positions that are narrow, parochial, or prejudiced. The officials must themselves determine the weight that should be attached to an argument, on account of its intrinsic merits or the power wielded by its proponents.

The "private-regarding"[19] motives of interest groups was observed in the urban renewal context. For example, in Madison Park some of the church groups were afraid of losing clientele and favored low-income housing in the area for that reason. The civil rights groups similarly made no reference to low-income housing but expressed enthusiasm for the possibility of a racially balanced school. The views of poor communities are likely to reflect a self-interest and a parochialism that is a natural consequence of the pattern of their lives and of their lack of citywide contact. Three out of four Madison Park residents interviewed did not belong to any citywide organization.[20] Over one-half seldom read about Boston politics. Two-thirds *never* associated with friends outside of their neighborhood.[22] The percentage with low education was in each case significantly higher than that of those with more education.[23] It is hardly surprising, therefore, that in answer to the question "Would you prefer low-income housing in this neighborhood, or a citywide racially balanced school?" over half of those interviewed opted for the more parochial and self-interested alternative of low-income housing, with only one in five preferring the school.[24] Logue based his opposition to low-income housing on two "public-regarding" issues: that the school would be more profitable for the city and that the low-income housing would result in a racially segregated area.

Clearly the decision maker must act in the "public interest" and need not take into account parochial and private-regarding interests. We have seen, however, that to determine what the public interest is, is difficult.[25] To say how it ought to be reached is somewhat easier. If certain interests, because of their lack of access to bureaucracy, are excluded from official recognition, then this lack of access is likely to constitute an obstacle to the emergence of the public interest, however conceived.

Thus when the project director of Madison Park stated that the residents there were "not particularly the people to plan a high school with," he was ignoring the possibility that consultation with local interests, however parochial or private-regarding, could bring to light preferences and attitudes not considered by the planner, thus expanding the planner's own range of alternatives, and working out a plan that might eventually reflect an adjustment between competing interests.[26] In Madison Park the interests of local groups were finally taken into account because of the power of the groups to command attention. Their power was augmented by advocates sophisticated in the manipulation of technical and political tools and sensitive to the political context in which the BRA was operating.[27]

In February 1839, in response to a petition from over one thousand black women for the "redress of the wrongs done them and the evils they suffer,"[28] the Massachusetts House Committee on the Judiciary replied that since the abolition of slavery "no inequality of civil rights has here existed," and if a person were "deprived of any of the privileges of freedom and the excitements of ambition, or any of the enjoyments of social happiness, it is by a power beyond that of the laws."[29]

Subsequent analysis suggests that the power of the law to affect human behavior and attitudes is greater than that claimed by the house committee in 1839, although even the most ardent believers in the law's power would fall short of the serious claim that a legislative enactment could turn a man into a woman—at any rate legally.[30]

This study has attempted to discover the extent to which legal techniques might be effective in controlling administrative discretion. We have noted that both substantive rights and adjudicative and other consultative procedures contain many merits in this regard. They also, however, contain defects and a limited capacity to deal with certain problems. It has been suggested that an understanding of the limits of legal action ought to allow us to provide for the legal control of discretion in a manner that is sensitive to the nature of the administrative process and the constraints operating upon bureaucracy, and hence more likely to prove successful.

It has been suggested too that we ought to recognize the limits facing a bureaucracy's clientele to utilize substantive and procedural rights provided for their benefit. Again, recognition of the obstacles to access to bureaucracy, or to rights against bureaucracy, may assist in assessing the real opportunity to utilize machinery that is provided, and in removing obstacles to access (where it is possible to do so).

It bears repeating that the so-called public interest will not necessarily be served by proposals seeking to increase the power of parochial or narrow interests. Nor is it suggested that all who claim to "represent" any particular interest necessarily do so. It is suggested, however, that the "problems of the powerless" are such that their interests are often unlikely to be heard or, if heard, are not sufficiently loud or powerful to receive attention.

If decision makers are to be in a position to mediate the emergence of the "public interest," they ought at least to be cognizant of the existence of the spectrum of disparate interests and their intensity. Both substantive "rights" and procedures for participation are, in many situations, ineffective to guarantee this situation. Skilled advocates might assist, provided they understand the plural nature of the public interest, the political nature of the administrative process, and the limits of legal action.

Legality, Advocacy, and Bureaucracy

Notes

1. P. Selznick, *Law, Society and Industrial Justice* (1969).
2. By Victor Thompson [*Modern Organization* (1961)], who attributes the reasons for this behavior to organizational structure and heirarchy.
3. See M. Shapiro, "Stability and Change in Judicial Decisionmaking: Incrementalism or State Decisis?" 2 *L. In Transition Q.* 134 (1965). In this article Shapiro applies to judicial decisionmaking theories expressing this view adopted by R. Cyert and J. March, *A Behavioral Theory of the Firm* (1963), and D. Braybrooke and M. C. Lindblom, *A Strategy of Decision* (1963). Nonet suggests that the "effective administrator" will "typically" seek to reconstrue a rule as a policy directive. In practice, however, the attempt becomes frustrated by internal and external pressures for consistency. P. Nonet, *Administrative Justice* at 246-247 (1969). Chester Barnard notes that coordination of activities in organizations requires the avoidance of formal orders except on routine matters and in emergencies. Most rules "are in effect formal notice that all is well—there is agreement, authority is not questioned." C. Barnard, *The Functions of the Executive*, at 126 (1966).
4. M. Edelman, *The Symbolic Uses of Politics* (1964).
5. J. Q. Wilson, "The Strategy of Protest: Problems of Negro Civic Action," 3 J. Conflict Resolution 291 (1961).
6. Five of the 12 cases where appellants were represented were successfully appealed; 25% of other cases were successfully appealed.
7. For example, in one case the worker did not inform the client, at the time barely subsisting while awaiting the answer to her DA application, that she was eligible for unemployment security benefits. In four other cases the appellant learned at the hearing that items such as surplus food, summer camp grants for her children, heating, etc., were available to her. A report on Massachusetts welfare revealed that clients on GR were rarely given help when the caseworker could have "done a few obvious things to help the clients establish their eligibility," National Study Service, *Meeting the Problems of People in Massachusetts*, chap. 11, p. 8.
8. Nonet [*Administrative Justice* (1969)] claims similar results for the "organizational advocacy" of the unions with regard to claims for workman's compensation benefits in California.
9. Fair Housing, Inc., referred eight of the nine complaints alleging discrimination in the purchase of a house.
10. "It is the policy of Fair Housing to locate housing only in stable, integrated or predominantly white neighborhoods" (*Semi-Annual Report, Fair Housing, Inc.*, at 4, (1963). Complaints referred to the MCAD from other sources show no specific patterns.
11. H. Gans, *The Levittowners*, at 312 (1967). See also J. Cohen and R. Robson, "The Lawyer and the Legislative Hearing Process," 33 *Nebraska L. Rev.* 523 (1954), where the authors refer to the function

of a legislative hearing as allowing the public to "blow off steam" and to provide "window dressing" for a decision on a bill reached prior to the hearing.

12. See S. Plager and J. Handler, "The Politics of Planning for Urban Redevelopment: Strategies in the Manipulation of Public Laws," *Wisc. L. Rev.* 724 (1966), for an account of the "political and planning skills" that can be imparted to groups low in political influence.

13. We are reminded of this fundamental point by T. Parsons, "On the Concept of Political Power," in R. Bendix and S. Lipset, eds., *Class, Status and Power*, at 240 (1966). *Contra*, R. Dahrendorf, *Class and Class Conflict in Industrial Society*, at 169 and *passim* (1959). Compare Hart and Sacks' "fallacy of the static pie," *The Legal Process*, at 111 (1958).

14. See E. Banfield, *Political Influence*, at 338 (1961).

15. S. Alinsky, *Reveille for Radicals* (1966). Although Alinsky believes that "the only way that people can express themselves is through their leaders." See his p. 87.

16. L. Peattie, "Drama and Advocacy Planning," 36 A.I.P.J., 405, 406 (1970).

17. See M. Edelman, *op. cit.* Michael Lipsky has referred to ways additional to the dispensing of symbolic satisfaction by which organizations satisfy their "reference publics." These are token material satisfactions, internal innovations and organization, and the postponement of proposed action. Lipsky, "Protest as a Political Resource," 62(4) *Amer. J. Polit. Sci.* 1144, at 1155-1156 (1968).

18. N. Long, "Power and Administration," in F. Rourke, ed., *Bureaucratic Power in National Politics*, at 14 (1965).

19. E. Banfield and J. Q. Wilson, "Public-regardingness as a Value Premise in Voting Behavior," 57 *Amer. Polit. Sci. Rev.* 4 (1964).

20. Seventy-six out of 102 interviewed.

21. Seventeen out of 102 read no papers ever. Of the remaining 85, 44 stated that they read about Boston politics or political news "sometimes" or "almost never." The other closed response offers were "usually" (9) and "always" (31).

22. Thirty-five out of 102. Over half (56 out of 102) associated with their neighbors less frequently than several times a year.

23. For example, 57% (21 out of 37) of those with fewer than eight years' schooling never associated with people outside of their neighborhood, as compared with 23% (9 out of 35) of those with a high school education.

24. Fifty-four preferred the housing, 23 the school, and 25 (24%) had no preference.

25. See M. Meyerson and E. Banfield, *Politics, Planning and the Public Interest*, at 323 (1955), where the authors point out that the public interest is not a "unitary" concept, but is plurally determined.

26. Banfield describes this process as "social choice," where "each actor seeks to attain his own ends; the aggregate of all actions—the situation produced by all actions together—constitutes an outcome for

Legality, Advocacy, and Bureaucracy

the group, but it is an outcome which no one has planned as a 'solution' to a 'problem.' It is a 'resultant' rather than a 'solution.' " E. Banfield, *Political Influence*, at 326-327 (1961).

27. See L. Keyes, *The Rehabilitation Planning Game* (1969). Keyes deals with the BRA projects in Boston's South End, Charlestown, and Washington Park. Keyes views the urban renewal process as a game which is "basically a political one in which the LPA bargains with the project area citizens over the nature of the proposal to be developed for their neighborhood." See his p. 7.

28. "Report on Sundry Petitions Respecting Distinctions of Color," Mass. H. No. 29 (1839), in *Tracts on Slavery*, ed. Harvard College Library (1874).

29. *Ibid.*, p. 6.

30. "De Lolme's remark that Parliament can do anything except make a man into a woman and a woman into a man is often quoted. But, like many of the remarks which De Lolme made, it is wrong. For if Parliament enacted that all men should be women, they would be women so far as the law is concerned." I. Jennings, *The Law and the Constitution*, at 170 (1958).

Index

Index

213